If I'm Jewish
and You're Christian,
What Are the Kids?

✦ANDREA KING

If I'm Jewish and You're Christian, What Are the Kids?

✦ ✦ ✦ ────────────────────────────

*A Parenting Guide
for Interfaith Families*

Foreword by Alexander M. Schindler

UAHC Press ✦ New York, New York

Library of Congress Cataloging-in-Publication Data

King, Andrea.
If I'm Jewish and you're Christian, what are the kids? : a parenting guide
for interfaith families / Andrea King ; foreword by Alexander M. Schindler.
  p.   cm.
Includes bibliographical references.
ISBN 0-8074-0452-7 (alk. paper): $10.00
1. Intermarriage—United States.   2. Interfaith families—United States.
3. Children of interfaith marriage—United States.   4. Jewish families—
United States—Religious life.   I. Title.
HQ1031.K53   1993
306.84'3—dc20   93-24708
                                                                          CIP

This book is printed on acid-free paper
Copyright © 1993 by the UAHC Press
Manufactured in the United States of America
10 9 8 7 6 5 4 3 2

This book is dedicated
to the memory of
Nathan's Jewish grandparents,
Morris and Sylvia.
I hope they would be proud.

why to transmit religious values to their children are, in fact, common to most Jews. She thus reminds us, as we have repeatedly learned over the past fourteen years, that "outreach" and "inreach" are fundamentally the same—that we in North America are *all* constantly "choosing" Judaism, having to re-affirm our faith and make room for it in our lives.

By reporting the experiences of couples and children who live with the numerous dilemmas of interfaith family life, King brings the issue home to us. As we listen to the searching voices in this book and as we recognize our own stake in their concerns, we experience a deepening of our *mentshlichkeit*, that feeling of identification with other human beings that is the very foundation of love, marriage, parenthood, and Judaism.

Rabbi Alexander M. Schindler, President,
Union of American Hebrew Congregations

♦ ♦ ♦ ————————————————————————

Acknowledgments

My first and biggest thanks must go to the scores of interfaith families who shared their stories through formal interviews, in small group discussions, or informal chats with me. I am especially grateful to the interfaith couples who were willing to talk about issues that they had not yet resolved. Their openness provided an honest look at the problems that intermarried parents face. My thanks to the children of intermarriage who helped me write this book. Their candid thoughts and feelings were indispensable. I also want to acknowledge the grandparents who spoke with me about the choices that their intermarried children made and their feelings about those choices. I am indebted to them for their willingness to talk about what was often a painful subject.

Among the people who deserve special thanks are those who read successive drafts of this book and contributed their insights: Lydia Kukoff, former director of the Outreach Department for the Union of American Hebrew Congregations, who first suggested that I write the book; Dru Greenwood, current director of Outreach; and Bethany Gilbert, an intermarried parent who is living with the choices and decisions that the book describes. To Aron Hirt-Manheimer, my editor, who encouraged and guided me, I extend my heartfelt thanks.

Thanks also to the Women Writers Computer Group of Los

Angeles, whose support never faltered through the lengthy process of producing this book.

Finally, my love and thanks to Ben and Nathan for their incredible patience. In many ways, this book is as much theirs as it is mine.

◆ ◆ ◆ ──────────────────────

Introduction

I never thought I'd be a Jewish mother. Few Episcopalians are.

I grew up in a family that was identifiably but not fervently Christian. I had a baptism, attended Methodist and then Presbyterian Sunday school, and went to church camps and vacation bible school. I joined the Episcopal church as a teenager, drawn by the richness of its liturgy and rituals. The church provided me with a loving, supportive community that shared my theological and political views.

Most of the men I dated were Christians. Several of them were members of my church. I began to envision a church wedding and imagined what being part of the Young Married Couples group would be like. I pictured my children's baptisms, and I assumed that I would someday teach Sunday school.

Then I met Ben. He was born at Brooklyn Jewish Hospital and had been raised in a modern Orthodox home. Although Ben did not belong to a synagogue, he was intensely interested in events and ideas that affected the Jewish people. Until he met me, he had never dated a church-going Christian.

From the beginning of our relationship, we both understood that neither of us was going to change. Within a month, we knew we would marry. We also knew that the difference in our religions would not make our life together easy.

We began to learn about each other's religion. Ben stayed

home from work on Rosh Hashanah and Yom Kippur, and I celebrated Christmas with my parents and siblings. I had the privilege of meeting Ben's favorite rabbi, and Ben got to know my parish priest. Most Sunday mornings, Ben sent me off to church with a cheery "Have a nice pray!"

Gradually, I began to appreciate the strength of Ben's ties to his Jewish heritage. He felt a personal connection to Jewish history. He looked for Jews and Jewish achievements in books and newspapers and experienced a shared sense of accomplishment. When we watched the movie *Hester Street*, Ben recognized facets of his parents' childhood in the movie's depiction of life on New York's Lower East Side in the early 1900s. These were his people; he was one of them.

In contrast, I represent a second generation of native Californians. No one in our family knows for sure when our ancestors came to this country, and as far as I have observed, none of my relatives retains any vestige of European culture. Apparently my English, German, French, and Irish forebears were all Protestants who heartily embraced America and American ways. The only sense of ethnic heritage or identity I felt was that of the generic American Protestant. Ben's strong sense of cultural identity was unfamiliar to me.

Shortly after marrying Ben, I began my work in early childhood education. Observing children and assessing their growth as a preschool teacher, director, and consultant, I came to understand how important a sense of identity is to young children. Because I am a Christian married to a Jew, I have been especially interested in the children of intermarriage and how they view themselves and their place in the world.

Through the years I have talked with interfaith couples whenever I could, learning as much as possible about how they raised their children. I have asked intermarried parents how they chose their children's religion. I have observed and listened at length to children of intermarriage as they struggled to establish their identities and personalities.

By the time Ben and I were ready to have a child, I had been working with young children and their parents for almost ten years. Most of the intermarried parents I met had told their children they were half-Christian and half-Jewish, or that they were both. Many of them followed a four-holiday calendar, celebrating Christmas and Chanukah, Easter and Passover. Their Jewish/Christian children tended to know something about both religions but did not feel they belonged to either one.

I also knew a few interfaith couples that had chosen to practice just one religion as their family faith. I observed that those children who had a clear religious identity often demonstrated a level of self-esteem that seemed to be absent in children who had an ambiguous or mixed religious identity. The single-religion children felt a sense of community with their religious group. They looked forward to the holidays and life-cycle ceremonies of their faith, often measuring their growth by their participation in those events. They frequently exhibited an especially strong sense of family unity and bonding during holiday seasons and life-cycle celebrations, but they also had friends of other faiths. I came to realize that the children of intermarriage benefit from having a single-religious orientation.

Two years before our child was born, Ben and I chose Judaism as our family religion. Although neither of us wished to convert to the other's faith, we did want to function as a homogeneous unit, participating together in rituals, holidays, and life-cycle events.

We chose Judaism because Ben very much wanted our child to feel that he was part of Jewish history and culture. Although the spiritual aspects of Judaism were not very familiar to me, I felt that the Jewish worldview, with its emphasis on justice, freedom, and responsible action, would provide a solid moral foundation for raising a child. I also thought that spiritual matters were private, and I trusted that my child would work out his own relationship with God.

Moreover, I was certain that Ben would reject the idea of raising our child as a Christian. I was far more comfortable with the idea of being a Christian within a Jewish family than Ben was with being a Jew in a Christian family. Theoretically, I had no problem with my child being a Jew, and I felt that the synagogue could serve as a community of shared values and as a support system for our whole family.

Then, as now, my Christian beliefs represent personal convictions and do not diminish the respect I have for Jewish traditions, tenets, and culture. I recognize and enjoy Judaism as a way of life. Jewish ethical, moral, and philosophical teachings do not conflict with my private religious creed, which I have no compelling need to bequeath to my child.

What was important to me was that our child have a solid religious background and education, as well as a system of beliefs and values that would provide him with moral support throughout his life. For his part, Ben wanted our child to be Jewish but not necessarily religious.

After hours of discussion and debate, including talks with a rabbi we both respected, we agreed that the only way our child would grow up feeling and knowing he was Jewish was if we participated in Jewish rituals, holidays, and life-cycle events and if we entered into Jewish community life, which included membership in a synagogue. Ben was not enthusiastic about rejoining organized Judaism. Nonetheless, he braced himself for the experience, realizing it was necessary in order to accomplish the goal of instilling our child with a Jewish identity.

Recognizing the traditional view that Jewish identity passes from mother to child, we decided it was important that our child be formally converted to Judaism. We learned from the local Orthodox rabbinic council that they would not sanction nor even recognize our child's conversion because, in their judgment, it would be impossible for us to raise a Jewish child if I did not convert. Our experience was not unusual. The reaction of Orthodox Judaism to intermarriage and interfaith families is often icy disapproval. Accordingly, we planned a Reform conversion ceremony, to be performed when our child was one year old.

Before our child was born, we told our families and friends, including my priest and fellow-church members, of our decision. We made it clear that our child would be Jewish—not half-Jewish and half-Christian, not Jewish/Christian, not Christian and Jewish during alternate years, but Jewish. As a result, no one was surprised to get an invitation to Nathan's *berit* and *pidyon haben,* and no one asked when he was going to be baptized. Our life as a Jewish family had begun.

From the beginning, we told Nathan that he is Jewish and that we are a Jewish family. When he was an infant, we introduced him to Shabbat observances and Jewish holidays. When Nathan was one year old, we had a conversion ceremony for him. Three Reform rabbis met us, our friends, and our families at the beach on a gray day in May. After the appropriate pledges and blessings had been made, Nathan was gently immersed in the Pacific Ocean, and everyone celebrated with a potluck picnic. We started taking Nathan to Shabbat services regularly when he was two, and at three he helped select the *mezuzah* (a small case containing a Hebrew passage from the Bible) that we mounted on his bedroom door frame. The next year, he started religious school at the Reform synagogue that we had joined.

Although Nathan knew that some of his relatives were Christian, we waited until just before his fourth birthday to tell him that I am not Jewish. We based our timing on his ability to handle paradox. Until then, Nathan, like all very young children, had thought in absolutes. When we knew that Nathan was able to consider two dimensions of a situation simultaneously, we decided that he was ready to handle the knowledge that I am not Jewish. One night, as we all sat together after dinner, I said, "Nathan, you know that Grandma Virginia and Grandpa George are Christian?"

"Yeah," he replied. "They have Christmas and stuff."

"Well," I continued, "when I was growing up in their house, I celebrated Christmas, too. When I was a kid, my parents raised me as a Christian."

"But you're Jewish now," Nathan said.

This was the hard part. "Well, actually, I'm not," I told him. "I'm still a Christian. I'm a Christian person living in a Jewish family."

Nathan quickly responded, "Then I'm half-Jewish and half-Christian."

"No, you're not," replied Ben. "Mommy and I thought that it would be too confusing for you to be both Jewish and Christian, so we decided that you would be Jewish and we would be a Jewish family, even though Mommy isn't Jewish."

Nathan thought for a minute, and asked, "Why aren't you Jewish, Mommy?"

"Because Grandpa George and Grandma Virginia are Christians, and when I was little, Grandma and Grandpa raised me and my brother and sisters as Christians," I replied.

"Why are Grandpa and Grandma Christians?"

"Because when Grandpa George and Grandma Virginia were children, they grew up in Christian homes with their parents, who were my grandmas and grandpas, and they were all Christians."

"Why were all your grandmas and grandpas Christians?"

"Because their mothers and fathers were Christians."

"Why were their mothers and fathers Christians?"

"For the same reason—because their parents were."

This line of questioning continued and covered several generations. Then Nathan began to categorize all of his relatives and friends according to their religion. "Is Richard Christian or Jewish? Is Rebecca Christian or Jewish? Aunt Bonnie's Jewish, right? What about Dan, the ice-cream man?"

I knew that pointing out similarities and differences is typical four-year-old behavior, and I wasn't worried that Nathan would reject his non-Jewish friends. He was simply reordering his world, using the new information he had just acquired.

Later that week Nathan said, "Mom, I know what happened at the beginning of time."

"Really? What?"

"At the beginning of time, there wasn't just Adam and Eve. There had to be Adam and Eve and another man and woman, too."

"Oh?"

"Yeah. At the beginning of time, there had to be one Jewish man and woman and one Christian man and woman. That's why we have both kinds now."

For him, that was the only explanation for the way things

were. I decided to let his conclusion go unchallenged for the time being. I knew he would soon discover that the world also has other religions. In addition, I knew that it would be a few years before he would be ready to learn that Christianity has its roots in Judaism.

A few days later, Nathan again suggested that he was half-Christian and half-Jewish.

"No," I said, "you're all Jewish."

"How can I be? You're not Jewish."

"Because Daddy and I decided that you're Jewish, and that's what you are. Remember those pictures in your scrapbook of the party at the beach when you were little? That's when Daddy and the rabbi dipped you in the ocean, and you were converted so that everyone would know you are Jewish. And you are."

"But you're Christian, right? So if you're Christian, why do you celebrate Chanukah and not Christmas?"

"I celebrate Chanukah with you and Daddy and our Jewish friends and relatives because we are a Jewish family. But privately, I also celebrate Christmas because it's important to me in a special way."

He considered this for a moment. "Well, Mom," he said, "then *you're* half-Jewish and half-Christian."

"Well, Nathan," I replied, "I guess you're right."

Nathan was finding his own explanation for a perplexing situation. A few months later, he put another piece into place. While Ben and I spent a weekend away, Nathan stayed in my sister's home, where one of the main attractions was her finches. Watching them, Nathan asked his aunt, "Marianne, do you think your finches could mate with our parakeet?"

Knowing that four-year-olds are avidly interested in where babies come from, she didn't flinch. "Probably not," she answered. "Usually animals only mate with their own kind."

"Not always," he pointed out. "Sometimes they can mate with different animals, and that's how we get new animals—like when horses mate with donkeys to make mules."

"That's true."

"So maybe it could work," he persisted. "Maybe your finches

could mate with our parakeet, and we could get a new kind of bird."

"Well, maybe," Marianne agreed.

Nathan was quiet for a minute or two. Then he asked, "Did you know that my mom celebrates Christmas in her heart?"

"Oh?" Marianne was surprised by this sudden change of topic. "Does she?"

"Yes, because she's half-Jewish and half-Christian. But," he continued, "when my mom mated with my dad to make me, her entire body was Jewish, and that's why I'm all Jewish."

Nathan had found a way to explain and confirm his Jewishness.

Nathan has had many opportunities to learn about Christian holidays and life-cycle events from my extended family. He has attended Christian weddings, baptisms, and funerals. Every year at Grandpa George's house, Nathan and I help decorate Grandpa's Christmas tree. Nathan participates as a guest in Christian festivals without experiencing confusion about his role or his identity. In that context, Nathan is the Jewish member of a Christian family.

We were fortunate to find a local Reform congregation with a high percentage of interfaith families. Soon after we joined, I was asked to combine my training in parent education with my personal experience to lead a series of discussions for intermarried couples. As I worked with interfaith couples, I found that they were often uncomfortable with their handling of holidays, family rituals, and their children's religious identity. Yet when many of these couples tried to discuss religion, they ran into monumental roadblocks. Because religion is so intertwined with the best and worst of their own childhoods, many of them find it very difficult to discuss. Couples often limp along for years saying, "We've got to talk about it someday." For many, that "someday" never comes.

There is a strong tendency for interfaith families to practice a little bit of each parent's religion. I am often asked, "Why shouldn't we combine the best elements of Judaism and Christianity in our family life?" It seems to me that exposing children to elements of two religions rarely gives them the sense of identity, the emotional security, and the consistent moral code that a single positive religious affiliation provides.

Some couples protest, saying, "We've been doing Christian and Jewish holidays for several years now, and everything's fine." I do not argue with them. The first six years or so are usually easy for the family that combines two faiths. Before the age of about six, children do not question the validity of belonging to two religions. They enjoy having a dual-religious identity, celebrating two sets of holidays, even attending both church and synagogue. The two-religion plan works when the children are small, but in a few years, they will ask questions, such as How can we be both Jewish and Christian? and Do we believe in Jesus or not? Their real question is, Who am I?

The path that I consider the most beneficial for the children of intermarriage may not be feasible for all interfaith parents. The couple that cannot agree on one family religion may decide that their only option is to combine Christianity and Judaism. If neither parent can accept the idea of raising the children in the other parent's faith, the couple may conclude that avoiding the issue of religion altogether or choosing a third or "neutral" religion is the best course of action. These options are not discussed in this book, however, because in my experience, most interfaith couples either choose one religion or try to blend Judaism and Christianity.

◆ ◆ ◆

Chapter 1

Introducing Two
Interfaith Families

- What options are open to interfaith couples?
- What are the most common choices made by interfaith couples?
- What factors do interfaith couples take into account
  in deciding their children's religious identity?

Introduction

Today, intermarriage is not the outrage that it once was. Except in extreme cases, parents who disapprove of marriage
outside their faith are unlikely to disown a child who intermar-
ries. Jews who "marry out" are not as likely to be accused of
rejecting their Jewish heritage or of trying to gain entry to a
Christian-dominated society. Many contemporary lay and religious leaders recognize intermarriage as a natural result of living in an open society.

Very few major Christian denominations officially condemn
Jewish/Christian intermarriage. While the Roman Catholic and
some Orthodox Christian churches strongly discourage marriage outside the faith, the leaders of most mainstream Christian sects in the United States do not consider marriage between their members and Jews to be a serious problem. Many

Protestant clergy will perform intermarriages without requiring that the children of these unions be raised with a particular religious orientation.

In contrast, intermarriage remains a topic of grave concern to the organized Jewish community. Some Jewish leaders fear that intermarriage will lead to the eventual demise of the American Jewish community. They point out that historically the Jewish home has been the center of religious ritual and observance, and they maintain that unless *both* parents are Jewish, their home cannot be a genuinely Jewish one. Many Jewish leaders contend that the children of intermarriage are lost to Judaism. This constitutes a significant loss since a little over one half of all American Jews intermarry.

Intermarriage is discouraged by the organized Jewish community, and many Jews are highly critical of the practice. However, some of the more liberal segments of American Judaism have begun to search for ways of adapting to the reality of intermarriage. The Reform movement has developed an Outreach program and policies designed to include intermarried couples and their children in congregational life.

Intermarriage no longer automatically excludes a family from participation in a religious community. Even when neither partner converts to the other's religion, the interfaith family can worship together. But how do interfaith couples answer the age-old question "What about the children?"

But What about the Children?

At some time, every interfaith couple is asked the above question. Friends and relations, even total strangers, want to know how the couple plans to resolve their religious differences as they prepare to become parents.

Some interfaith couples tackle the question head-on. They discuss, research, negotiate, and make plans. Some of them choose either Christianity or Judaism as the family faith. Others find original approaches to the problem: They decide to celebrate Christian and Jewish holidays in alternate years; they plan to raise their first child in one faith and their second in the other; they choose to observe both religions in equal measure; they decide not to choose an official family faith.

Many interfaith couples find that confronting the subject of religion is too difficult. They avoid talking about religion and drift into a patchwork pattern of family rituals without ever deciding how to address their religious differences.

No matter which route a couple takes, their decision (or lack of one) has both immediate and long-range consequences. Children's feelings about themselves and their family, their heritage, and their community are influenced by the choices that their parents make.

Two Family Models

Just as no two families are identical, no two interfaith families handle the issue of religion in precisely the same way. Nevertheless, several common themes emerged during my talks with intermarried parents and their children. Interfaith families generally take one of two approaches:

- They choose either Judaism or Christianity as the family faith.
- They observe some holidays and rituals from each religion.

The two families introduced in this book are composite portraits, drawn from my personal observations, formal interviews, informal conversations, and discussion groups. Each family's story is told through a compilation of actual characteristics, comments, and anecdotes.

The statements, explanations, feelings, reactions, and events presented in this book are true and were revealed to me over a ten-year period by scores of interfaith families. However, their names and other identifying information have been changed, and their accounts have been combined for the sake of simplicity.

Sam and Kathy Cohen: Choosing One Faith

The frame of Sam and Kathy's front door has an enameled brass mezuzah. There are silver Sabbath candlesticks on the sideboard, a Jewish calendar in the kitchen, and a Hebrew school schedule on the refrigerator. Theirs is clearly a Jewish home, even though Kathy is not Jewish.

"I guess we're not a typical family," says Sam. "I'm Jewish, our sons are Jewish, but Kathy is not. Our way of life is a little different, but it's worked for us—at least, so far."

Sam and Kathy, eight-year-old Danny, and five-year-old Zeke are an interfaith family that is functioning exclusively within one religious tradition. They observe Jewish holidays and celebrate Jewish life-cycle events. The boys are getting a Jewish education. Kathy is a full participant in the Jewish aspects of their family life. She even serves on the parents' committee of the boys' religious school.

"Some people think it's odd that I agreed to have our sons raised as Jews and that I am so involved in their Jewish upbringing," Kathy says. "It doesn't seem so strange to me. It seems like the best plan for us."

After many long discussions, Sam and Kathy decided that theirs would be a Jewish family. "We explored all the options," says Kathy. "Before we had Danny, in fact before we even got married, we talked to as many interfaith couples as we could and listened to their stories. Some were pretty interesting. One of the families we talked to started out practicing Christianity and Judaism in alternate years. They said that things went along all right until their son was about six. That December, he asked when they were going to get the Christmas tree, and his mother said, 'Don't you remember? This is the year we celebrate Chanukah.' And the boy replied, 'Aw, do we *have* to be Jewish this year?' To him, being Jewish was a big disappointment that happened every other year. After that, the family pretty much gave up on Judaism. Their story helped convince me that practicing both religions was a bad idea."

"To me, it was just a matter of common sense," says Sam. I fail to see how any one person can be half-Jewish and half-

Christian, no matter what your parents are or what intellectual. rationalizations you use. Christians and Jews think and act differently. Neither way is necessarily better than the other, but they're different. You can't be both a Christian and a Jew."

"We felt," Kathy continues, "that if we were going to raise our children in only one religion, one of us had to make the decision to participate in the other's religion. Maybe having the boys practice Christianity wasn't as important to me as having them practice Judaism was to Sam."

Danny and Zeke have no doubts about their religious identity. "Some of the kids at school say that I'm half-Christian because Mom is Christian," Danny says. "But I tell them that I'm all Jewish. They start believing me when I tell them that we don't have a Christmas tree."

Keith and Sari Grayson: Practicing Both Religions

"Of course we practice both religions," Sari says. "I wouldn't ask Keith to give up Christmas any more than he would ask me not to attend a seder. We want our kids to have the best of both religions."

"They have Christmas and Chanukah every year, as well as Easter and Passover," says Keith. "We brought two religions to this marriage, and our kids get the benefits of both."

Sari and Keith are among the interfaith couples that have chosen to include elements of both Christianity and Judaism in their family life. "We think this is the most logical way to handle a mixed marriage," says Sari. "We know other couples who have done really far-out things. One couple decided that their boys would be Jewish and their girls would be Christian. They had three girls before they finally had a boy. I'm not sure that they had planned to have four kids, but they had to keep trying until they had at least one boy. Another couple decided that their first kid would be Jewish, their second Christian, and so on. They divorced after two kids—what a mess. The court battle centered around something called 'spiritual custody.' And several families we know celebrate Jewish and Christian holidays in alternate years. It seems to work for some of them, but it would make me schizophrenic. I think our decision is the best."

Sari and Keith's children—Hannah, age sixteen, Charles, age twelve, and Heather, age seven—are growing up with the understanding that they are both Christian and Jewish. "We're lucky," Heather says. "We get Christmas presents *and* Chanukah presents."

Sari and Keith occasionally take the children to religious services, but the family does not belong to a church or synagogue. "We're not particularly religious, but we want the kids to know something about their roots," Sari says. "Besides, if we belonged to a church, we'd have to belong to a synagogue, too. That would be too much."

Holiday traditions in Sari and Keith's home include decorating a Christmas tree and exchanging Christmas gifts, lighting the menorah on the eight nights of Chanukah, hunting for eggs on Easter morning, and hosting an Easter brunch. "On Passover, we usually go to my mother's house for the first seder," explains Sari. "Sometimes we have the second seder, and sometimes my sister does."

"But when we have the seder," Keith says, "we keep it non-religious. We don't read the traditional script. Last year, for instance, we talked about homeless people. And one year, we attended a feminist seder at which all the Jewish heroines throughout history were discussed. We try to make the seder relevant to our life."

The children's reactions to their family traditions vary according to their age. The thoughts about religion expressed by seven-year-old Heather are predictably concrete. "I'm really glad that I'm Jewish and Christian," she says. "We do Mommy's holidays and Daddy's holidays. And we get one present every day during Chanukah and lots of presents on Christmas."

Twelve-year-old Charles is in the process of trying to define the family's religious identity. "Well, Mom's Jewish and Dad's Christian, so we're both. But we're not like those Christians who go to church all the time. And we don't stay home from school on Jewish holidays or go to Hebrew school. We just celebrate the holidays of both religions. It doesn't have anything to do with beliefs."

When asked to comment on his religious beliefs, Charles answers, "I can't tell you what I believe about God, but I feel that people should be honest and have high morals just because that's what's right, not because of religion."

Hannah, the sixteen-year-old, has definite opinions about religion and her parents' decision. "I know Mom and Dad will tell you that they raised us half-and-half because we celebrate Christian and Jewish holidays. They say we're Jewish *and* Christian, but actually we're neither. Look, if we were Christian, we would have had baptisms and first communions or confirmations. If we were Jewish, I would have had a bat mitzvah like my Jewish friends and cousins. In fact, Grandma Sadie said that she'd give me a bat mitzvah if I went to Hebrew school, but I didn't go because I didn't want to hurt my dad's feelings. Now I feel like I'm missing out on something."

Reminded that she can have either a baptism or a bat mitzvah at any time, Hannah sighs, "Yes, but I'm talking about what I'm missing *now*."

Comments

It should be noted that other family options might have been included in this book. Among them are deciding against any religious affiliation, choosing a religion other than Judaism or Christianity, and raising children as Christians.

It is not uncommon for an intermarried couple to resolve the question of how to raise their children by deciding that religion will play no part in their family life. When a couple chooses this option, they usually will have no affiliations with a church or synagogue, their children will not have a formal religious education, and their family will not observe religious life-cycle events. Most no-religion families develop secular celebrations of Christmas and Easter, in accordance with the Christian orientation of our society. The children of a no-religion interfaith marriage grow up feeling that they are part of mainstream America. Their families look and act like the majority of families around them.

A small number of interfaith couples choose to join a faith other than Christianity or Judaism. For instance, they may become Unitarians, Quakers, or Zen Buddhists. Others may choose a third religion rather than confront the issues that arise from their disparate outlooks. But whenever couples opt for a religion out of compromise rather than conviction, the adopted faith may be too tenuous to form the basis of a lifelong and intergenerational religious commitment.

Although a significant number of intermarried couples choose Christianity as their family faith, no such family is included in this book. Instead, Sam and Kathy Cohen, who chose Judaism, represent all families that choose one partner's religion as their family faith.

Many of the issues that the Cohens confront and discuss would be the same if had they had chosen Christianity. These issues include the desire to give their children a clear religious identity, to celebrate one set of holidays together, and to commit their time, energy, and financial resources to one religious institution.

Some issues, however, would be significantly different for Sam and Kathy had they chosen Christianity because the family that chooses Christianity does so for different reasons with different results.

Interfaith couples that practice Christianity have chosen to be part of the majority culture in our society. These couples often say, "It's just easier this way." Children of intermarriage who are raised as Christians generally do not have to adjust to being part of a minority group in public school and in the community.

Choosing Christianity often allows an interfaith family to blend into the community more easily. It is a more comfortable option for those who dislike drawing attention to themselves by being different from their coworkers, friends, and neighbors. The fact that one parent is Jewish almost ceases to be an issue.

When an interfaith family chooses Christianity, the Jewish parent often feels guilty, even if he or she is not observant. Many nonpracticing Jews are concerned about the future of the Jewish people. They want their children to identify with Jewish causes, Jewish people, and the nation of Israel. Because Judaism encompasses both a religion and a culture, many Jews value their ethnic heritage (art, music, literature) as highly as they do their religious identity. Even if the Jewish parent doesn't feel strongly about passing on Judaism's religious tenets, he or she is apt to want the children to understand and take part in Jewish culture. The non-Jewish partner rarely feels as guilty as the Jewish one does about not passing on his or her religion.

Functioning as a Jewish family, the Cohens remain outside the mainstream of American society in some ways. And, since Kathy has not converted to Judaism, the family does not automatically fit into the Jewish mainstream. In fact, because intermarriage is viewed as a threat to Jewish continuity, the Cohen family may encounter resentment and even hostility from some Jews, despite Sam and Kathy's commitment to raise their children as Jews. Unlike the interfaith couple that chooses Christianity, Sam and Kathy may not be able to blend inconspicuously into the community.

Reform Judaism is making an attempt to address the needs of intermarried families like the Cohens. As acceptance increases and more support becomes available, choosing Judaism is becoming a more viable option for interfaith couples like Sam and Kathy.

This chapter has provided a brief overview of the choices made by the Cohen and Grayson families. In the next chapter, each couple describes how they met, married, and made their decision about how they would address the issue of being an interfaith family.

✦ ✦ ✦

Chapter 2

Before the Children

- What adjustments do interfaith couples need to make after they marry?
- How do the partners' backgrounds and extended families affect lifestyle decisions?
- How do interfaith couples decide on their children's religion?

Introduction

Never has it been as easy for Jews and Christians to meet, fall in love, and marry as it has been in the second half of the twentieth century in America. Christians and Jews live in the same neighborhoods, go to the same schools, work together, and belong to many of the same civic, social, and political groups. Despite some parents' protests, interreligious dating and marriage are everyday occurrences.

Interfaith couples all say that meeting and falling in love are the easy parts. It is when these couples begin to consider marriage that questions that never even occur to same-faith couples arise and differences begin to emerge. Interfaith couples can take no decision for granted, from which foods to serve at the wedding reception and the kind of ceremony they will have to the religious education of their unborn children.

Sam and Kathy Cohen

"We talked about religion from the first day we met," says Sam. "Religion was one of our major topics of conversation for months."

"Because we were friends before we started dating, the subject of religion was never off-limits," Kathy points out. "We talked and argued about religion, politics, education, economics—everything. It wasn't until we had discussed all the really important issues that we decided to start going out."

Sam and Kathy met while working on a community project. They soon discovered that they shared many ideas and values, despite their religious differences.

"Our religious views are very different," says Sam. "Although Judaism is a religion, I see it as my cultural identity. To me, being Jewish has to do with actions, not beliefs. I grew up in a fairly Orthodox home: My family kept kosher, my father went to synagogue every day, and so on. My parents also conveyed the message to me at an early age that we were lucky to be Jewish. They would tell me about the great Jewish thinkers, scholars, musicians, and scientists. They did not say that Jews were better than anyone else—just that we were fortunate to be Jewish. It made me feel special, but it had nothing to do with religion.

"By the time Kathy and I met," Sam continues, "I had left organized Judaism. I was Jewish, but I chose not to affiliate with Jewish groups. I considered myself more of a cultural than a religious Jew."

"I never thought of my religion as a culture," says Kathy, "and I was never particularly passionate about being Presbyterian. My religion is personal and private. It took Sam a long time to accept that I wasn't going to try to convert him."

Early in their relationship, Sam and Kathy realized that their religious differences were a potential problem. "We both had our own religious identities," says Sam. "We both valued our roots, and neither of us wanted to give them up. But when we got serious about each other, we realized that we couldn't even plan a wedding without considering our different backgrounds and values."

Sam and Kathy both realized that marrying outside their faith meant they would each have to change some of their expectations of marriage. "I always expected to marry a Christian," says Kathy. "That's one of the reasons Sam and I didn't date right away. We became friends because we didn't see each other as potential mates. When we started talking about getting married, we had to take a serious look at what we wanted, beginning with the wedding ceremony itself.

"For instance, I had always imagined having a church wedding, but for Sam that was out of the question. I found it hard to let go of my fantasy—the candles and flowers on the altar, the traditional wedding march, and everything else. I felt that loss for a long time."

"I also had some ideas about what my wedding would be like," Sam interjects. "I had always expected to be married by a rabbi, under a *chupah*. But we couldn't find a rabbi who would marry us because Kathy's not Jewish, even though by that time we had decided to raise our kids as Jews. So there went my vision as well."

"The wedding part was disappointing to both of us," says Kathy. "I felt that I was making a commitment to the Jewish community, and it wasn't willing to accept me. It made me mad. Anyway, we ended up being married by the college chaplain in the music room of the college, which was fine. Our friends and families came. We had Renaissance music and we served cake and champagne in the campus rose garden. The wedding was nice, but it wasn't my ideal nor Sam's."

"I always took it for granted that I'd marry a Jewish woman," says Sam. "Although I didn't go out of my way to meet and date Jewish women, I envisioned myself living in a Jewish household and raising Jewish kids with a Jewish wife. I also expected my wife to have primary responsibility for making a Jewish home, but marrying Kathy meant I had to change my ideas. I've had to take a much more active role in creating a Jewish family than I thought I would play. It's a lot of work!"

How did their families react to their decision to marry? "Well, my parents were not thrilled when I decided to marry Sam," says Kathy. "They were sure that our religious differences would create problems. They used what I have since learned is a classic line: 'Marriage is hard enough without complicating it by marrying someone who is so different from you.'

"In addition," Kathy continues, "they worried about my leaving the church if I married Sam. As it's turned out, this fear of theirs was justified. I'm not involved with any church now, although I do go to church a couple of times a year."

"My family was concerned that you *would* continue to be involved in the church," says Sam. "They weren't happy about the possibility that their grandchildren might be baptized and that sort of thing."

Kathy continues, "My parents also worried that I would experience culture shock because of our religious differences. But I told them that I was confident I could handle the situation. Because I felt sure that we knew what we were doing, I ignored their protests.

"Of course, I was sorry that they didn't jump for joy," continues Kathy. "I guess that was another part of my fantasy about getting married—that my mom and I would plan the reception and go shopping for the perfect dress and that my family and my fiancé would like one another. None of that happened. My parents weren't crazy about Sam, and they had their doubts about our marriage. Maybe they'd have had a similar reaction if I'd married a Roman Catholic or a Hispanic or an Asian or anyone else who was different from me. In the beginning, they maintained a certain distance, making me feel very uncomfortable. The tension didn't subside for a long time—not for years."

"By the time Kathy and I met," says Sam, "my parents knew that I was intent on making my own decisions and that they would not be able to change my mind. They would have preferred that I marry a Jewish woman, but they didn't reject Kathy. Because Kathy never proselytized or even talked about her religion, it didn't become a sore point."

"I think that when our families realized that we were going to get married anyway, they accepted the fact," says Kathy. "I remember they gave us some advice, but neither set of parents interfered either before or after we got married. And they've become more accepting over time."

Sam and Kathy spent hours discussing as many aspects of child rearing as they could think of. "We talked about education, discipline, what children should eat, where children should sleep, what kinds of vacations families with young children should take—you name it," says Kathy.

Sam adds, "We also talked about what our children's religion would be."

"We realized that religion was a positive thing for both of us. We wanted our kids to have the same appreciation for their religious heritage and the same warm feelings about religious traditions that we had about ours," Kathy says. "We briefly considered practicing both Christianity and Judaism, and we talked with several couples who had chosen to do that. But we decided against it. We both felt that we had each benefited from having a strong, consistent religious background, and we wanted the same thing for our children."

Before they were married, Sam expressed a strong desire to have their children raised as Jews. "Being Jewish is very important to me," he says. "Having children is also very important to me, and I cannot imagine my children not being Jewish. I knew that being Christian was part of Kathy's identity, but she had never talked about whether she wanted our children to be Christians. I hesitated to bring the subject up, but it was too big an issue to avoid."

"We both knew that we had to talk about it," says Kathy. "I was pretty sure that Sam wanted our kids to be Jewish. What was important to me was that they have a solid grounding in a religion whose values I embrace. I wanted my kids to have meaningful traditions, holidays, ceremonies—things like that. And I wanted them to feel that they belonged to a religious community. Of course, I had always just assumed that my kids would be Christian, would have Christian holidays, and would belong to a Christian church. I had to confront the prospect that our kids would have a solid religious background, but it wouldn't be Christian."

"I wasn't so sure that I wanted my kids to have a *religious* background," Sam points out, "but I knew I wanted them to be Jewish. Finally, I just said it straight out."

"It was a relief to have the subject brought into the open," says Kathy, "so that we could start talking about what it would mean."

And what did it mean? "First of all," says Kathy, "it meant that my kids would be different from me. It meant that there are things that I had been brought up with that I would never share with my kids. I had to think about that for a long time before I could get comfortable with the idea.

"Then one day," Kathy recalls, "we were eating in a Greek restaurant. We were listening to wonderful Greek music and watching the waiters dancing. And Sam said, 'If for some reason I couldn't be Jewish, I'd like to be Greek.' It was then that I realized how important and special being Jewish is to him. I thought, If we raise our children as Jews, they'll have that special feeling, too. After that, I started looking forward to being part of a Jewish family and raising Jewish kids.

"Next, I had to face the fact that raising the kids as Jews meant giving up my traditions and adopting Sam's. Since we wanted our kids to understand fully that they were Jewish, they had to live in a Jewish home. That meant no baptisms, no Christmas tree, no Easter eggs. I knew that we would not succeed in raising our children Jewish if I observed a different set of rituals and holidays than they did. That wouldn't make any sense. Still, I went through a period of sadness, almost of mourning, for what I was about to leave behind and give up. Even though I knew something else was going to replace my former traditions, I couldn't help feeling sorry for myself."

"I know that Kathy misses celebrating her Christian holidays," says Sam. "In December, she sometimes watches *Miracle on 34th Street* or *It's a Wonderful Life,* and I see her getting teary-eyed about Christmas."

"I like Christmas, and it took me a while to get used to the idea of not having Christmas in my home," Kathy says. "It was hard to give away my Christmas ornaments. I ended up lending them to my sister. I go to see them on her tree each year.

During the first few years, I felt sad seeing them there, but now I can genuinely enjoy them.

"You know," Kathy continues, "many people assume that I just gave in and said to Sam, 'Fine, whatever you want.' But it wasn't like that at all. We made a joint decision to raise our children as Jews. It was not a compromise, and I didn't relinquish my right to choose. I still maintain my own religious beliefs. I don't feel bad about not passing them on to the kids, but I do feel a little schizophrenic at times."

For a few years after their marriage, Kathy continued to be an active member in her church. Says Sam, "It never bothered me that Kathy belonged to her church, and once in a while, I'd even go with her to an event or a service. All her church friends were nice people, and I know she enjoyed the relationships she had formed there. I, however, did not wish to get more involved."

Before Sam and Kathy had children, they maintained their separate religious identities. "I never expected Sam to go to church with me," Kathy says. "I went on my own and had my own friends there. And for the first few years we were married, before we had the kids, I decorated a little Christmas tree, a live one, and kept it on the front porch."

"Actually, I was never comfortable with the Christmas tree, even though it was on the porch," recalls Sam. "I was glad when it finally died. I recall asking Kathy not to replace it."

"Because I understand Sam's discomfort with Christian ideas and images, I never decorated the house for Christmas," Kathy says. "But I continued to carry on my own traditions quietly, like putting a lot of effort into choosing just the right gifts for my parents and going to church with them on Christmas Eve."

"And I went to High Holiday services," says Sam. "I think we both went to my parents' house for seders, didn't we?"

"Yes, we did," Kathy recalls. "I figured I'd better learn about such things if our kids were going to be Jewish."

"I didn't realize it at the time," says Sam, "but our decision to raise our kids as Jews also meant that I had to get involved in organized Judaism again. Eventually, it dawned on me that

Kathy couldn't raise Jewish kids single-handedly, and it was up to me to provide the strong Jewish influence in the family. I wasn't keen on the idea of joining a temple, but we did. Maybe if Kathy had been Jewish, we wouldn't have belonged to a temple or sent the kids to Hebrew school or participated in so many Jewish activities. Since she's not, we have to make an extra effort to provide a Jewish environment for the boys. I never imagined that I would be a gung-ho Jewish father, but that's the way it turned out. When you make a commitment, you have to act on it."

Keith and Sari Grayson

"When Sari and I met," says Keith, "we didn't spend much time discussing religion because she is not particularly religious and neither am I. She didn't say, 'Let's go to temple,' and I didn't say, 'Let's go to church.' "

Sari continues, "When we were dating, we talked about our childhoods, like everyone does. But we talked about childhood holidays more than about religion. Keith told me about how wonderful his Christmases were, and I told him about seders and Chanukah. It was part of the getting-to-know-you process, but not a big part."

"And we didn't discuss religious beliefs at all," explains Keith, "because neither of us was into that."

Sari and Keith met at a folk-dancing group. "It was love at first sight," Sari says. "But we dated for a long time before we got married. We didn't want to rush things."

As Keith and Sari became more serious about each other, they talked about practicing both Judaism and Christianity in their family life. "I told Sari that I couldn't imagine December without the kind of Christmas I grew up with. My mom always baked holiday cookies, we had a huge tree, and, of course, we exchanged gifts. We always got new clothes at Easter, and we had a big Easter egg-coloring party. I wanted my kids to have those experiences."

"It was hard for me to accept all that," says Sari. "Christmas and Easter were holidays that other people did. Even though

I'd always been slightly jealous of the kids who had Christmas, I couldn't see myself setting up a tree or painting Easter eggs in my home. On the other hand, I could understand why Keith wanted to continue his traditions. I certainly didn't want to give up my Jewish holidays just because Keith didn't celebrate them."

"That's why we decided to observe aspects of both religions," says Keith. "We didn't want to give up anything."

"I grew up in a very Jewish home," says Sari. "We belonged to a Conservative congregation, and even though we didn't follow all the customs, there was never any doubt that we were a Jewish family. I love Jewish holidays, rituals, and ideas. They're very meaningful to me, and I didn't want to give them up. I want my kids to have the same kind of memories that I do."

"Our family was Protestant but not affiliated with a particular denomination," says Keith. "Because we moved a lot, we usually joined whatever church was in the neighborhood. I went to Episcopal, Methodist, Presbyterian, and Congregational Sunday schools. I guess it was more of a social than a religious involvement—a good way to get to know people in a new community. What was important was that we as a family had our own holiday traditions that never changed."

Keith's parents did not object to their engagement. "My folks liked Sari right away," says Keith. "They didn't care that she was Jewish. But my father did take me aside and say, 'I hope this doesn't mean that the children will be Jewish.' I replied, 'No, they'll be both.' That satisfied him."

"My parents were definitely upset," says Sari. "When we announced our engagement, they began a kind of cold war. They did not say anything against it outright, but they sent me books and magazine articles that discussed the higher divorce rates and difficulty fitting in socially that intermarried couples supposedly had. I got phone calls from friends of my parents telling me horror stories about their children's intermarriages. I'm sure my parents put them up to it. I know they want Jewish grandchildren. They're concerned about the survival of the Jewish people, and so am I. But Keith is the only person I ever wanted to marry, and it just so happens that he's not Jewish.

Our engagement caused a lot of strain between my parents and me."

"Some of Sari's other relatives also gave her a hard time," Keith says. "They said things like, 'Think about what you're doing to the Jewish people. What about the Holocaust?' They put her on the spot."

"Because I had never been a troublemaker or a difficult kid, they were surprised," says Sari. "I also wasn't used to being the center of controversy, and I hated it. Finally, I gave up trying to justify my decision and stopped talking about it. We invited everyone to the wedding and hoped they'd come.

"When my parents realized that the wedding was going to happen," Sari says, "they changed their approach. They started suggesting, in not-so-subtle ways, that Keith should convert."

"My parents didn't care if Sari converted to Christianity or not," says Keith. "But if I had converted to Judaism, they'd have had a fit."

"Frankly, neither of us felt that the other one had to convert," says Sari. "It just wasn't an issue for us."

Keith and Sari were married in an outdoor ceremony by a minister friend. "We didn't want a wedding that was identifiably Christian or Jewish," says Keith. "We wrote our own service, using parts of both ceremonies plus other things. It made a good balance."

"But we didn't have a *chupah*," says Sari, "and Keith didn't break the wineglass. My family was very disappointed."

"It wasn't a Jewish wedding," Keith points out. "Doing those things would have turned it into a Jewish ceremony. I mean, we didn't mention Jesus either, because that would have made it a Christian ceremony. We deliberately excluded any religious symbols and traditions."

Before they had children, Sari and Keith established a few of their own family traditions. "The first year we were married," Sari relates, "Keith brought a Christmas tree home, and a part of me said, 'This is not Jewish. You don't do this.' But for years I had secretly longed for a Christmas tree, and now here it was, in my own living room. I loved it, and I felt guilty for loving it. I had such mixed feelings about it."

"Sari told me about Chanukah, although we didn't celebrate it before we had the kids," says Keith. "But every spring, even before we had the kids, we went to Sari's mother's house for a Passover seder. After the kids were born, we sometimes had a seder here."

Keith and Sari did not discuss beforehand whether having children would change the traditions they had established. "We didn't talk about it because we never did anything religious before the kids were born," says Sari. "We didn't belong to a synagogue or a church. At Christmas, we had a tree, we exchanged presents, and I baked my mother-in-law's famous Christmas cookies. We had never had a crèche and had never attended Christmas Eve services. Going to my mother's for the seder was the only Jewish thing we did on a regular basis. I guess we both assumed we'd just continue doing the same things after we had kids that we had been doing before."

"Before we got married," says Keith, "we decided that we wanted our kids to have the best of both religions, the parts that we enjoyed the most from our own childhoods."

Sari says, "My parents thought that exposing the kids to both religions would really confuse them, and we talked about that possibility. But to us, it seemed like the most natural thing to do. We decided that our children would be fine."

"What we wanted was for them to be exposed to both Jewish and Christian influences without being immersed in either," says Keith.

"We never sat down and formally agreed on which holidays we would celebrate," says Sari. "We just started celebrating both Christmas and Chanukah. Keith had always celebrated Christmas and after the kids came along, I wanted to start celebrating Chanukah."

"The first year we were married, we also hosted an Easter brunch," says Keith, "and it has become a family tradition."

"At Passover, we go to my mom's for the first seder," says Sari. "It's very important to me. Then we sometimes have the second one here."

"We never felt we had to decide in advance which holidays to celebrate," says Keith. "We felt comfortable just letting it happen."

Sari and Keith think that their solution is a good compromise. "How could we possibly practice just one religion?" asks Sari. "Keith would be hurt if I insisted on only Judaism, and I'd be furious if Keith pushed too hard for Christianity. Neither of us wants to create that kind of struggle."

"It's like food," says Keith. "I like Chinese and Sari likes Italian, so we go to both kinds of restaurants. We don't always do my thing, and we don't always do her thing. The same with religion. We do both. It's fair, and everyone's happy."

Comments

During the childless years of an interfaith marriage, a couple usually finds ways to respect and adapt to each other's religious needs and habits. For instance, while Sari was able to accept having a Christmas tree in her home, Kathy decided not to decorate her house for Christmas. Some interfaith partners maintain their own religious identities and practices, like Kathy, who occasionally attended church after she and Sam married. For some couples, compromise comes easily. Sari and Keith, for example, decided with a minimum of discussion that their children would be exposed to the "best of both religions."

Interfaith couples often develop a delicate balance of holidays, rituals, and religious practice, based on their backgrounds and emotional needs. They assume that having children will not upset that balance. Sari and Keith, for instance, never discussed which holidays to celebrate. They developed holiday observances that included two holidays from each tradition: Christmas and Chanukah, Easter and Passover. As Keith says, "What we ended up doing didn't seem to require a definite decision. We felt comfortable just letting it happen."

Few interfaith couples go into marriage thinking that no problems will arise. Some develop specific strategies for addressing problems; others expect that most difficulties will eventually resolve themselves. In both instances, the birth of a couple's first child often upsets many of their plans and expectations.

◆ ◆ ◆ ──────────────────────────────

Chapter 3

The Advent of Children

- How does having a baby change an interfaith couple's relationship?
- Should a couple decide their baby's religious identity in advance?
- After the baby is born, are most couples able to implement their plan?

Introduction

Most interfaith partners are able to adapt to each other's religious ideas, practices, and needs—up until the time that their first child is on the way. Then the future, as well as the past, takes on a fresh significance for first-time parents. The new baby represents a bridge between what has been and what will be. Half-forgotten memories of childhood events and feelings loom large in the minds of parents-to-be. Religious and cultural themes acquire a new importance. Spouses who have allowed each other to live and let live are often overpowered by the need to pass along their own childhood traditions and beliefs to their child.

These strong feelings can take intermarried spouses by surprise. Many couples who had previously decided that "religion is no big deal" find themselves heatedly discussing religious rituals. Those who thought they would "face certain problems as they come up" are suddenly forced to confront them. A parent who has made a commitment to raise the children in the other parent's religion may question and reexamine that decision, heightening the level of tension that often accompanies the anticipation of the birth of a child.

The intermarried couple's best insurance against unexpected, traumatic reactions to their baby's birth is to reach an explicit, mutually satisfactory agreement about child rearing before the child is born.

Sam and Kathy Cohen

Despite Sam and Kathy's decision to raise their children as Jews, the birth of their first son aroused some anxiety, particularly on Kathy's part.

"I felt confident that our decision was the right one," says Kathy, "but I also had to take a long, hard look at what it meant for both the child and me. I had to accept the fact that I would have to explain again and again why my child is Jewish and I'm not and that I would sometimes find it confusing to do so."

"Some of her relatives came right out and said they thought that raising our child as a Jew was a lousy idea," Sam recalls. "They asked her, 'Why Jewish? Why not Presbyterian? Why do *you* have to make the sacrifice? Why not Sam?' "

"It was hard to explain," says Kathy. "By the time the baby was on the way, I had gone through months of soul-searching and I was feeling good about raising our child Jewish, but I found it hard to describe how I felt to my relatives. They were dealing with the issue on an emotional level, while our decision seemed so logical and rational. Getting emotional about the subject just made it harder to discuss."

"I think that's because you were having a hard time justifying the decision to yourself emotionally," Sam suggests. "As long as the subject was being discussed intellectually, you could handle it. I think you avoided the emotional issues because they made you uncomfortable."

"It was a hard decision," Kathy says. "I resented getting grilled

at his grandparents' house when he was just a few weeks old, it struck me that we had made a commitment to this child and to the Jewish community. We had made a personal decision on one level, but it had much wider ramifications."

"After the seder, my father was holding Danny," Sam recalls, "and he guided the baby's hand under the napkin where he had hidden the *afikoman*. He pulled out the *afikoman* and said, 'Look, Daniel found it! Give him the prize!' You could see how much introducing his grandson to Jewish traditions meant to my father."

Keith and Sari Grayson

"We've always agreed that we wanted our kids to have the best of both Christianity and Judaism," says Keith. "But beside celebrating all the holidays, I had never really thought about what that meant until the kids were born."

Like many interfaith couples, Sari and Keith discussed the issue of childbirth rituals for the first time just before their first child was due. "I had assumed that our kids would be baptized," says Keith. "We hadn't talked about it before, but it seemed to me that if we were going to bring the kids up in both faiths, we would have the new-baby ceremonies of both religions, including baptism."

Sari had objected. "If you baptize a baby, you're making it a member of the Christian church," she says. "We agreed to raise the kids in both religions, not make them members of one. When Keith started talking about baptism, I said something like, 'Well, then, if it's a girl, we'll take the baby to the synagogue and have a baby-naming ceremony, too. And if it's a boy, we'll also have a *berit*.' "

"My point was," Keith continues, "that baptism has no religious meaning to Sari one way or the other. So having the kids baptized shouldn't have been a problem for her. Frankly, it would have been fine with me if we had had a baby-naming ceremony in a synagogue, too. A *berit*, well, that would have been going a little too far."

"I think we were both a little surprised that this issue became a problem," says Sari. "We had agreed to raise the kids in both religions, and I was comfortable with the idea. But when it came to baptizing them, I just couldn't agree. And Keith vetoed circumcision. So we ended up doing nothing."

"I guess you could say that we hit an impasse when it came to new-baby ceremonies," says Keith. "But that was years ago. We're beyond that point now."

Comments

Intermarried couples that have made definite plans for their children's religious upbringing can minimize the difficulties that accompany the birth of a first child. The Cohens had a clear plan for their children's religious identity. As Kathy comments, they were used to the idea of being a Jewish family by the time their first child was on the way. Because they had frankly discussed the issue of a family faith, Sam and Kathy were able to acknowledge and confront their individual reactions to Danny's birth. Both Sam and Kathy trusted the decision they had made, and both followed their plan.

The biggest surprise for Kathy was that her in-laws and the community warmly welcomed Danny and included her in the traditional Jewish ceremonies. Kathy's experience is not uncommon. Jewish parents who had previously treated their child's non-Jewish spouse indifferently frequently greet the birth of a grandchild with unreserved joy, particularly if the intermarried parents are willing to let the child take part in Jewish rituals. It often takes the birth of a grandchild for Jewish in-laws to accept their Gentile son- or daughter-in-law.

The Graysons had decided to give their children the best of both religions and to address problems as they arose. However, when their first child was born, they could not agree how to celebrate. The probable course of action would have been to celebrate with birth rituals from both faiths. But neither parent was at ease with a new-baby ceremony that was part of the other parent's religion. Despite the Graysons' intention to include the best of both religions in their family life, none of their three children was formally welcomed into either parent's religious community.

Keith and Sari's experience is typical of that of couples "who have decided to raise the children both." On a theoretical level, these couples are comfortable with the concept of including holidays and rituals from both religions. This solution seems logical, democratic, and even fun. Having decided on "both," these couples rarely discuss the issue in greater depth. They tend to assume that both partners have the same ideas about how the family will celebrate holidays and life-cycle events.

When the first child is born, couples who have chosen "both" often discover, as Keith and Sari did, that they have conflicting ideas about how to integrate the traditions of both religions. Like many other intermarried Christians, Keith assumed that his children would be baptized and that their baptism would be acceptable because his Jewish partner would not care one way or the other. Sari's strong negative reaction perplexed him, especially since he had offered to have the children named in the synagogue as well, although he considered having a *berit* too Jewish.

Sari, who regarded baptism as a public statement of identification with Christianity, assumed that their children would not be baptized. To Sari, baptism was a significant rite that could not be balanced or offset by a Jewish baby-naming ceremony.

Like many couples, the Graysons had avoided discussing the specifics of what raising their children "both" would mean. Consequently, when their first child was born, they were surprised by their strong and disparate responses. Their compromise solution was to do nothing.

Chapter **4**

◆ ◆ ◆ ────────────────────

When the Children Are Small

- When does religion start to play an important role in a child's life?
- How does religious identity affect self-concept and self-esteem?
- What effect do family rituals have on a child's developing self-concept?
- How do young children begin to develop a values system?

Introduction

In the first five years of life, a totally dependent infant becomes an autonomous person, with a mind, will, and ideas of her own. Just as important as the physical and intellectual skills she gains during the preschool years is her self-concept, the image she develops of herself.

The self-concept or self-image formed by a young child generally persists into adulthood. The way she sees herself at about age four becomes the basis of her self-image throughout life.

Self-concept is the result of two complementary sets of information. The first consists of *given attributes*—characteristics that are determined by biology, history, and other accidents of birth. Gender, ethnicity, physical traits, birth order, innate talents, and other given factors usually do not change throughout life. The givens in a child's makeup might include possessing long legs and gray eyes, being the firstborn, and having Irish ancestors.

The second set of influences on self-concept are *acquired attributes*—the skills, behaviors, and attitudes that an individual learns. Acquired attributes develop and change continually throughout a person's lifetime. An acquired attribute can become part of a child's personality through repeated exposure to certain ideas or experiences. For instance, a child may acquire a lifelong love of reading because her early childhood included being read to in a warm, nurturing family setting. Attributes can also be acquired through a child's conscious identification with a person or group. The child who takes up her grandfather's hobby may do so not only because she enjoys the activity but also because she wants to be like the grandparent she admires.

Family rituals greatly influence a child's developing identity. A repeating cycle of familiar holidays and life-cycle celebrations gives the child a sense of security and stability.

Despite the fact that interfaith couples bring two complete and often conflicting sets of rituals to their relationship, holidays and life-cycle celebrations may not pose a problem during the first years of a marriage. Many interfaith couples do not find it important to decide which family rituals to observe until their first child reaches preschool age. At that time, they may both be surprised by the strength of their urge to pass along to their child the rituals of their own childhoods. The influence of the extended families and the pervasive Christian messages around them create additional challenges for intermarried couples trying to decide on their family observances.

Religion and Self-Concept

Young children are generally interested in religion. In nursery school and child-care programs, children compare notes on their respective religions. Four-year-olds are often aware of who is Jewish, who celebrates Christmas, and who goes to Sunday school. Five-year-olds confidently explain that "Christians be-

lieve in Jesus and Jewish people don't." Although their understanding of theology may be limited to a concept of God as a
divine superhero, preschool children often discuss God, Jesus,
heaven, and Bible stories. They role-play weddings and funerals without grasping the religious significance of these rituals. Preschoolers apply religious labels to themselves and others in an attempt to classify and understand their world.

How does a child know which religious label to apply to herself? Many families regard religious affiliation as an inherent
factor of a child's identity. The child is born into a religion,
which becomes an established, dependable part of her life. She
participates in the holidays and rituals of that religion and re-
gards herself as part of a community that extends beyond her
family. For such a child, religion is as natural and as fixed as
is her gender or eye color.

Parents who view religion as a given send a message not
only to their child but also to their extended family and the
community. By declaring that their child is a member of a particular religion, these parents are asking that others treat the
child accordingly. From infancy, her religious identity is confirmed and supported by those around her. Friends might ask
a Jewish child if she will be reciting the Four Questions at the
Passover seder this year, or relatives might take a Christian
child to see a Christmas pageant. By treating religion as a given,
these parents insure that their child has a solid religious base.

When religion is a given, parents cite their family faith as a
reason for making certain choices or decisions. They will explain to their child, "We don't have a Christmas tree because
we're Jewish" or "We go to church on Easter because we're
Christians." Although she may not yet understand the theology or ethical core of the family faith, the young child is learning about aspects of her religious tradition as they affect her.

Other families regard religious identification as an acquired
attribute, something a child learns as she grows. They give the
child fewer overt messages about religion and assume that she
will form her religious identification by observing and participating in family, school, and community activities. The child
gradually draws her own conclusions about religious identity,

pursuing the issue when and if she is interested. The child of parents who see religion as an acquired trait usually absorbs the customs, beliefs, and values of the predominant religion of the community in which she lives.

Sam and Kathy Cohen

"We wanted our kids to know that they *belong* to a religion," says Kathy, "and that the traditions and values of the religion belong to them."

"There is also the cultural issue," Sam adds. "Judaism isn't only about what you believe. I want the boys to appreciate their cultural heritage, to know about Jewish ideas and history, to feel part of that. Since we don't live in a Jewish neighborhood, we're active in the temple. It gives the boys a sense of Jewish community. We also do many things to introduce them to Jewish traditions at home."

"We started observing Jewish rituals when Danny was born," says Kathy. "He had a *berit* and a *pidyon haben*. I'd never even heard of a *pidyon haben*. I learned that Danny, as a firstborn Jewish son, was supposed to be dedicated to service in the Temple. We had to use silver coins to buy him back symbolically from a member of the priestly caste. I found this ancient ceremony very moving."

"When Danny was a baby, we started celebrating Shabbat," says Sam. "We hadn't done that at home before he was born. But when he came along, it became important."

"I like going to temple services on Shabbat," says Zeke, "but what I like best is having Shabbat at home. Mom makes a big dinner, and we light the candles and say the blessings before dinner. And when we're away, we have these little candlesticks and candles that we light in our hotel or when we're camping or wherever we are, so we can have Shabbat anywhere."

"Our kids feel good about being Jewish," says Kathy. "It's part of their everyday life, not just something they think about on holidays. One day last summer, when Zeke was in an arts and crafts program at our local park, the children were making collages using shapes made out of construction paper. Zeke took two triangles, put them together and said, 'Hey, it's a Jewish star!' Suddenly all the kids were making them. And Zeke identifies with other Jews. For instance, Zeke has always liked Aaron Copland's music, but when he found out that Copland was Jewish, Copland went right to the top of Zeke's list."

"When Danny was four," Sam remembers, "we went into a department store and saw a singing Santa. The guy had an electric guitar and was singing upbeat versions of Christmas carols. He asked Danny which Christmas song he wanted to hear. Danny said that he was Jewish and didn't celebrate Christmas. The Santa said, 'Well, how about if I sing a song just for you?' And he sang 'Hava Nagila.' Danny was thrilled; he still talks about the singing Santa who did 'Hava Nagila' for him."

"At Zeke's nursery school," recalls Kathy, "there was a record player that the kids could operate by themselves. When I went to pick him up one day, the teacher told me that Zeke had put on a record at the wrong speed. It sounded slow and melancholy and strange. She was going to change it, but Zeke came running up with a big smile, shouting, 'Teacher, teacher! A Jewish song!' so she left it on. After that, the teacher got a few Jewish records."

Like most five-year-olds, Zeke defines who he is in terms of what he does. "We're Jewish because we do lots of Jewish stuff," says Zeke. "We go to temple and Sunday school, we have Shabbat and Jewish holidays, and me and Dan will have a bar mitzvah."

For Zeke, as for most children his age, holiday celebrations are the most tangible and visible elements of his religious identification. "In our family, we have Chanukah," says Zeke. "Every year we have a Chanukah party. Once our menorah fell over, and the house almost burned down! We have other Jewish holidays, too, like Passover and Purim and Rosh Hashanah. We go to Nana and Papa's [their Jewish grandparents] for those, or sometimes they come over here. But we don't have Christmas, because that's a Christian holiday."

Danny and Zeke participate in some Christmas festivities with Kathy's relatives. "I like Christmas at Grandma and Grandpa's house," says Zeke. "They have a Christmas tree, and we get presents, and Mom takes presents for everyone, even though it's not our holiday. Mom said it's like when we went to our friend Tai Wong's for Chinese New Year. We can go to his house and help him celebrate his holiday, even if it's not ours."

Zeke seems comfortable with the fact that Kathy is not Jewish. "Me and Danny and Daddy are Jewish," he says, "and Mommy's not. But she does Jewish things with us 'cause we're a Jewish family."

Because the family lives in a neighborhood that has few Jewish families, the boys are often the only Jews in their social and school groups. "Last December," Kathy recalls, "Zeke came home from kindergarten with a beautiful Chanukah picture— a blue menorah with flames of red glitter. He said, 'Everyone was making Christmas cards, so I made a Chanukah card.' I talked with his teacher later, and she said that it had been his own idea. She was embarrassed that she had introduced the activity as Christmas card-making instead of saying that the kids could make any kind of card they wanted."

"What makes me happy," says Sam, "is that Zeke did what he knew was appropriate for him to do as a Jew. He wasn't intimidated, and he didn't feel uncomfortable about it. He just went ahead and made a Chanukah picture instead of a Christmas card."

"There was another time," Kathy recalls, "when Dan was in kindergarten and the teacher put out old Christmas cards for the kids to use to make holiday decorations. There wasn't any choice. Danny's solution? He went ahead and made a Christmas decoration. By the time he brought it home, he had already decided what he wanted to do with it. He knew it wouldn't go up in our house but my folks would put it on their tree, which they did. In fact, they loved it."

Sam and Kathy are aware that Danny and Zeke, who are part of the tiny non-Christian minority in their school, might sometimes feel awkward, embarrassed, or out of step with their peers. "I grew up in a Jewish neighborhood," says Sam. "It didn't occur to me until I was ten or so that Jews are in the minority in our society. But my kids are faced with that fact every day."

"I grew up going to schools in which about one quarter of the kids were Jewish," says Kathy. "It was no big deal, and we Protestant kids sort of learned about Judaism by osmosis. But there are very few Jewish kids in the area we live in now. We're doing what we can to bridge the gap between our kids and the others, to make sure that the boys' friends know something about Jewish holidays and traditions."

When Danny started nursery school, Kathy spoke with the teacher about bringing Jewish holiday foods and traditions into the classroom. "She was very happy to have me do it," Kathy says. "Our nursery school had a strong parent-participation program, and the staff was very open to my suggestions. When we started, the only thing the teacher knew about Jewish holidays was that Jews light a menorah on Chanukah. I began with Rosh Hashanah, with the round challah and the apples dipped in honey, and we moved right through the calendar. On every holiday, I'd bring in a story and special foods, usually something the kids could help prepare. I kept it very simple when the kids were little: just the name of the holiday, a quick overview of the reason for the holiday, a story, and the food."

"When Zeke started nursery school," says Sam, "he went to the same school that Danny had attended. As soon as Kathy walked in the door with Zeke, the teacher said, 'Oh, great! Now we can have our Jewish holidays again!' Apparently, no one had done Jewish holidays with the kids since Dan had gone on to kindergarten."

Kathy points out that she was not trying to teach Jewish ideology to the other children. "I just wanted to familiarize the kids with some of the basic traditions and concepts that Danny and Zeke were growing up with. It's important to us that our children have friends who are comfortable with the fact that Dan and Zeke are Jewish."

"We don't want our kids to feel like oddballs," says Sam, "and we want their friends to have an accurate picture of Jewish traditions. That's why I am pleased that Zeke wants to have a Shabbat dinner for his birthday party. He's comfortable sharing that part of our life with his friends, and I think it's wonderful that they all want to come."

At religious school, the Cohen boys are being formally introduced to Jewish values and ethics. "Every week at religious school, we give *tzedakah*," says Zeke. "That's money we give to poor people. Last year, my class raised over a hundred dollars for poor people. Part of being Jewish is taking care of other people and taking care of the world."

"It's very important to me that the boys develop Jewish values," says Sam. "Doing religious rituals with the kids would be pretty pointless if we didn't explain and teach Jewish values at the same time."

Kathy says, "I knew that Zeke was beginning to understand some Jewish values last year when his school had a fair and I got the principal's okay to take the leftover food to our local soup kitchen. While Zeke and I were packing up the food, I explained to Zeke what the organization does and how much it depends on donations such as ours. After we had completed the delivery and were walking back to the car, Zeke suddenly stopped in his tracks and said, 'Mom! We did a mitzvah!' He was so pleased and proud. And I was proud, too. It was one of those moments that make me glad we had decided to raise the boys as Jews."

Keith and Sari Grayson

"We've always been up-front with our kids," says Keith. "We told them from the beginning that they're half-Jewish and half-Christian. They're completely comfortable with the idea and how we do things."

Seven-year-old Heather is at ease with her Jewish-Christian identity, describing herself in terms of both her parents' religions. "Daddy's Christian and Mommy's Jewish, so I'm both," she says.

Heather does not see any contradiction in being two religions. "Some kids at school say you can't be Christian and Jewish, that you could only be one. But I *am* both. They say that you have to believe in Jesus or not believe in Jesus. I never even think about Jesus."

When asked what it means to be Christian and what it means

to be Jewish, Heather answers, "If you're Christian, it means you celebrate Christmas and Easter and sometimes you go to church. And if you're Jewish, you celebrate Chanukah and some other holidays, and sometimes you go to synagogue."

"We try to take the kids to services now and then so that they'll be comfortable in both a church and a synagogue," says Keith. "It's important to know when to stand up and sit down, that sort of thing. Also, we want them to hear that the basic message is the same in both a church and a synagogue."

At age twelve, Charles looks back on his early childhood. "It never bothered me to be both religions when I was little. I remember thinking, 'Almost everybody is Christian, some people are Jewish, and I'm both.' The only thing that bothered me was that my parents and my relatives seemed to expect me to know about all the holidays of both religions, and sometimes they didn't explain them. I still can't figure out where the Easter bunny came from. But I didn't ask questions when I was little. I just enjoyed the candy and presents. It was fun celebrating all the holidays."

"Because traditions are very important to little kids," says Sari, "we observe as many as we can. Since holidays are basically family times, we try to celebrate them with our extended family. It seems like most holidays of all cultures involve a big family dinner—the only difference is whether you serve ham or matzah-ball soup. The one time that problems arise is when the holidays overlap. Sometimes, if Chanukah is too close to Christmas, it gets lost in the excitement, and we don't get around to lighting the menorah on all eight nights. But if Christmas falls during Chanukah, we usually just combine our holiday celebrations."

"We want the kids to understand the universal values that holidays celebrate," says Keith. "Instead of stressing the differences between the Christian and Jewish holidays, we look for the common ground. For instance, on both Christmas and Chanukah people give gifts, talk about peace and brotherhood, and focus on children. We don't talk about the religious aspects of any of the holidays."

Heather describes one of the family's Christmas rituals. "After we decorate the Christmas tree, we set up a little town under it, using tiny cars, houses, people, and real electric lights."

"We often add some Jewish decorations to our Christmas tree," Sari points out. "Last year, Heather's teacher taught the kids how to blow out eggs and decorate them for Christmas. Heather painted Jewish stars on some of hers. She was so proud of them."

Sari and Keith rely on their families to help them pass on holiday traditions. "My mom always has the first seder at her house on Passover," says Sari, "and we make sure the kids participate."

"At the seder, I got to ask the Four Questions because I'm the youngest cousin who can read," says Heather. "I read them in English, and my cousin Jonathan read them in Hebrew."

Sixteen-year-old Hannah also enjoyed growing up with two religions. "When I was little, it seemed as though I had the best of both worlds," she says. "I never felt left out because we celebrated all the holidays and went to church and to synagogue now and then. It was fun explaining to people that we were both religions. Once in a while, some kid would give me a hard time, saying things like 'How can you be two religions?' But my parents said we were, so we were. When I was small, it was no big deal. I didn't understand what a religion was anyway. It was just a matter of which holidays you celebrated."

"I want the kids to realize that there's not just one right path or one right idea," says Sari. "I want them to know that there are many ways of living a good life and that no one group is superior to any other."

"We talk about values a lot," says Keith. "We want our kids to develop basic Judeo-Christian values without their belonging to a specific religion."

Heather's youthful value system consists of absolutes. "You shouldn't do bad things," she asserts, "because it's wrong. If people do bad things to you, tell them to stop, and if they don't, you might have to hit them."

Keith and Sari teach their children values by setting an example. "We want them to be honest, so we try to be honest with them," says Keith. "We want them to be kind to other people, so we practice kindness. That kind of teaching always works better than preaching does."

"There's a poster that says children learn what they live," Sari states. "It says something like, 'If a child lives with love, he learns to love,' and so on. Well, we are trying to make sure our kids live with love and decency, and we hope that's the way they'll grow up."

Comments

Children learn about their religious identity from their parents' words, actions, reactions, and expectations. Zeke knows that he is Jewish because "we do lots of Jewish stuff." Heather confidently explains, "Daddy's Christian and Mommy's Jewish, so I'm both." Each child has successfully integrated his or her parents' message.

The Cohens regard religion as a given factor in their children's lives. At age five, Zeke has a positive image of himself as a Jew. At the same time, he feels comfortable sharing other people's celebrations because his mother has said that he and Danny could help them celebrate their holiday, "even if it's not ours." Zeke is young enough to accept with little debate what his parents say.

Sensitive to the fact that their children are in the minority in their community, Sam and Kathy are making an effort to foster tolerance among them and their non-Jewish classmates. Feeling that his classmates understand and accept him will help Zeke build confidence and self-esteem. His parents hope that Zeke will feel comfortable with his Christian peers.

Having embraced his parents' view of him as a Jew by birth, Zeke has begun to adopt Jewish values. When he and his mom took food to the soup kitchen, he felt the elation that comes from doing a good deed. That critical realization reinforced for him the fact that he is a good person. Furthermore, defining the act of charity as a mitzvah enabled him to integrate the Jewish values he is learning with his day-to-day life. It made him feel that he is not only a good person but also a good Jew.

Sam and Kathy have learned the importance of introducing

a vocabulary that helps the boys develop a value system. By providing labels for ethical principles (for instance, the words *mitzvah* and *tzedakah*), Sam and Kathy have helped their children recognize Jewish values as concepts, as actions, and as part of a larger worldview.

The Graysons have given their children the explicit message that they are half-Christian and half-Jewish. Keith and Sari consider having two religions an advantage. Having absorbed the message, Heather confidently proclaims her half-and-half status.

Are the Grayson children truly growing up with both religions? They were neither baptized nor named in a Jewish ceremony, and none of them has had any formal religious education. Although the family hosts a Passover seder and celebrates Chanukah along with Christmas and Easter, Keith says, "We don't talk about the religious aspects of any of the holidays." In the Grayson home, Christian holidays seem to take precedence. Chanukah is apt to get "lost in the excitement" when it falls too close to Christmas.

In this half-Christian, half-Jewish family, Keith and Sari minimize the differences between the two faiths. They point out the similarities in holiday celebrations, ethics, and philosophy, hoping that their children will understand that "the basic message is the same" in both religions. For Heather, the blurring of the line between Judaism and Christianity has so far resulted in a happy amalgam of holidays. For her, celebrating Chanukah is like having another Christmas. Her older siblings have memories of feeling equally comfortable with having been "both" when they were her age. As Hannah says, "It was just a matter of which holidays you celebrated."

Because young children generally accept their parents' statements uncritically, they are usually satisfied with the religious identity given them by their parents. When children of intermarriage are small, they are just as happy participating in one religion as in two. However, they usually find the next stage, middle childhood, more difficult.

Chapter 5

◆ ◆ ◆ _____

Middle Childhood

- How important is religion to the school-aged child?
- What questions does the school-aged child ask about religion?
- What role does peer pressure play in the school-aged child's religious identification?
- How do school-aged children develop a value system?

Introduction

A child's elementary school years are a time of exploration and expansion. As a school-aged child becomes more involved in school, sports, and social activities, his peer group starts to take on an increased importance. His focus begins to shift away from his family. More and more, he looks to his classmates for approval, acceptance, and standards of behavior. Parents know by heart the battle cry of the school-aged child: *"Everybody's doing it!"*

Along with developing his social, academic, and physical skills, the preteen is actively engaged in establishing his identity. He consciously compares himself with friends and acquaintances, gauging what he has in common with others and how he is unique. This is an important process. The school-aged child's self-concept depends partly on his perception of the similarities and differences between himself and others.

Although adults do not play as dominant a role in the school-aged child's life as they did in the younger child's life, they generally represent stability, constancy, and discipline. Parents, teachers, neighbors, and public figures serve as role models, both positive and negative.

During these years, a child needs adults whom he can rely on and who allow him to separate gradually, as he is ready. He needs the freedom to be both with adults and away from them. The preteen, like the toddler, uses adults as a base for emotional refueling before he strikes out again into his expanding world.

In his quest for independence and identity, the school-aged child may reject his religious training. He may be intensely interested in religious rituals and philosophy one year and completely apathetic or even hostile to them the next. Although he may complain about the religious practices that his parents observe and the values they espouse, his family remains at the core of his world, providing him with continuity and safety.

Sam and Kathy Cohen

"Life was certainly simpler when Danny was little," says Kathy. "We would tell him how things were, and he believed us. Now he questions everything."

At eight, Danny asks for proof, stands up for his point of view, and rarely lets a subject drop before he is satisfied.

"But to me," says Sam, "questioning everything and arguing about everything is a part of the Jewish tradition. It doesn't mean that he's rejecting us or our ideas; it just means that he wants to figure things out for himself. I respect that. I try not to cut him off; in fact, I encourage the questioning."

"For instance, when Danny started religious school, he was taught that Jewish men traditionally cover their head," says Kathy. "So he decided to wear a yarmulka at meals."

"He tried to get Zeke and me to follow his lead," says Sam. "I told him that it's fine for him to express his Judaism in that way, but it's not my way. It was a big issue for Danny for a couple of months, and we had many discussions about whether someone who ate bare-headed could be a 'good Jew.' Except on Friday nights, I never wear a yarmulka at dinner, but I respected Danny's wish to wear his whenever he wanted."

Because they know how important peers are to children of Danny's age, Kathy and Sam have made an effort to involve Danny with other Jewish children. "It's definitely a hassle to get up on Sunday mornings and take the boys to religious school," says Sam, "but it's the only chance they have to be with other Jewish kids."

"We want the boys to feel that they are part of a Jewish community, and that means being part of a group of Jewish children," says Kathy. "What they learn at religious school is important, but one of the main reasons we take them is to help them develop ongoing relationships with Jewish friends."

Danny's attitude toward religious school is slightly ambivalent. "What I don't like about Sunday school," he says, "is that we have homework. What I like is that I'm good friends with lots of the kids there. I also like our discussions. We talk about what's wrong in the world and what we can do to make it better. That's called *tikkun olam* in Hebrew, and it means 'healing the world.' It's really lots of things: cleaning up the environment, taking care of people who are homeless or sick or poor, ending war, working for freedom for everyone in the world. Doing all of those things is part of being Jewish."

Danny also attends Hebrew school one afternoon each week. "On the first day of Hebrew school," Danny recalls, "we got candy and doughnuts to show that learning is sweet. That's a Jewish tradition. I like learning Hebrew," he continues, "except that the class moves too slowly. It would be better if we went faster and played more games with Hebrew letters and words. It's pretty good when we play games."

Danny is conscious of being one of the few Jewish children in his public school class. "There's one other Jewish kid in my class; everyone else is Christian. Sometimes I feel kind of left out. One time, I got into a fight about Christmas and Chanukah, but that was the only time."

Sam explains. "One of Danny's good friends said that he

didn't think Chanukah was as good a holiday as Christmas, and I guess it just ticked Dan off. He popped the other kid, and they went at it."

"The teacher intervened immediately," says Kathy. "And she followed up with a class discussion about the importance of being sensitive to one another's holidays. The bruises healed right away, but the emotional hurt and the damage to the boys' friendship lasted much longer."

Most of Danny's peers accept and respect his religious affiliation. "Some of my friends even say they'd like to be Jewish because Mom makes being Jewish sound like fun when she comes to school and talks about the Jewish holidays."

Kathy has become adept at explaining the Jewish holidays. "Because our district has people from so many different countries and backgrounds, it has encouraged parents to come to the school and share their family's culture. Parents from Latin America, Southeast Asia, Russia—everywhere—have come to our kids' classes to talk about their heritage. So when I go in and talk about the Jewish holidays, it falls under the heading of 'multicultural curriculum.'

"It's worth doing," says Kathy, "even though it means I have to rearrange my work schedule. But let's face it, we always manage to find the time to do what's important to us."

Danny enjoys his mother's holiday visits to school. "It's always fun when she comes," he says. "But in a way, it's kind of weird that my mom talks about the Jewish holidays. Most of the kids in my class think she's Jewish. I guess she's sort of Jewish, because she knows so much about Jewish things."

Kathy has encountered some interesting responses from other children of intermarriage in Danny's class. "There are usually one or two students who will shout out, 'I know that! We do that at Grandma's house!' "

Danny says about the other children of intermarriage in his class: "Some kids in my class say they're half-Jewish. They mean that their mom or dad is Jewish and the other parent isn't. But they don't do anything Jewish. They do Christian things like celebrate Christmas, so I don't think they're half-Jewish at all. Besides, how can you be half-Jewish and half-Christian? You can't half believe in Jesus and half not believe."

Danny goes on. "I think that if you celebrate Christmas, you're Christian. If you have a Christmas tree and think that Santa Claus brings presents to your house, you're Christian, even if your mom or dad is Jewish. But if you just give people Christmas presents because *they* celebrate Christmas, that doesn't mean you're Christian."

What if a family celebrates both Christmas and Chanukah? "Well," Danny ponders for a moment, "I think that they don't really know what they are. They haven't thought about it very much, because Christmas is Jesus' birthday. It's like a birthday party for Jesus. And if you're Jewish, you don't believe that Jesus was the Messiah because the Messiah hasn't come yet. If you celebrate Christmas and Chanukah, you're saying that you believe in Jesus during Christmas and you don't believe in him during Chanukah. That doesn't make sense."

Although Danny is aware of his friends' religious affiliations, he did not choose his friends based on their faith. "My best friend, Jess, is Christian," Danny explains. "My second-best friend, Andrew, is Jewish. Third-best is a tie between Kevin, Owen, Mark, Rebecca, and Alan. Kevin, Mark, and Alan are Christian. Owen and Rebecca are Jewish. And then there's Richard, my pen pal from science camp. He's Christian."

Danny spent two weeks at camp last summer—one week at a Jewish camp and the other at a science camp. "I liked both, but I liked the science camp better," he says. "The Jewish camp was okay, but the food and the activities at the science camp were better. I liked the people at both camps the same. It was really fun to be in a Jewish camp with only Jewish kids. I want to go back to the science camp next year, and I want to go to a different Jewish camp—maybe one that's like a kibbutz, with farm animals that you have to take care of."

Although he enjoys spending time away from his parents, family times—especially holidays—are still important to Danny. "We always have a seder at Passover," he says, "and this year I read the Four Questions in Hebrew. I really read them; I didn't just memorize the words. Everyone in the whole family was there, and everybody read different parts. Of course, Mom's relatives read theirs in English. And Grandpa didn't know what the *afikoman* was when we were looking for it after the seder.

Then Zeke found it, and Grandpa said, 'I thought you said that was called matzah,' so we had to explain that the *afikoman* is matzah, but a special matzah."

Sam and Kathy are conscious of the amount of time they spend supporting their boys' Jewish education. "Besides Shabbat and holidays at home," says Sam, "there's religious school on Sunday mornings and Hebrew school on Tuesday afternoons. We also take the boys to services on Friday night once or twice a month. Kathy does the holidays in their classrooms about four mornings a year for each boy. I have monthly temple board meetings and spend time working at home on board business. Plus, we participate in various special events, such as Sunday school picnics, Purim carnivals, bake sales, and so on."

"Other parents ask me why I spend so much time doing Jewish activities with the boys and how I find the time to do so," Kathy says. "Those same parents spend at least as much time on soccer or music lessons or ice skating or gymnastics or something else for their kids. Sam and I feel that Judaism is an important part of the boys' lives, at least as important as activities like playing piano or ice skating.

"Danny says that I must be at least half-Jewish by now," Kathy continues, "and sometimes it feels that way to me, too. But at certain times, my Christian background asserts itself."

"For example," Sam explains, "Kathy and I have a disagreement about the need to apologize. To her, apologies are very important. I think it's because apologizing is related to the Christian concept of forgiveness. To me, making restitution is much more important than apologizing. Apologies are secondary."

"Sometimes our differences of opinion get in the way when we're dealing with the kids," Kathy says. "A couple of weeks ago, Danny was playing with Zeke's little car and broke it. He felt really bad, especially since he had not asked for Zeke's permission. He knew that Zeke would be mad at him. Danny was truly sorry. I felt that it would be enough if he apologized sincerely to Zeke and promised that from then on, he wouldn't use Zeke's things without asking. I knew Zeke would forgive him, and they'd be friends again. But the important thing to Sam was that Danny make a plan for replacing the car. To

Sam, Dan's feeling bad wasn't enough because it didn't get Zeke a new car. I think that saying you're sorry and hearing the other person say it's okay closes the matter, and you can then get on with your relationship."

"I think that first you have to make restitution to get past an incident and then you can get on with the relationship," Sam insists.

Danny remembers the incident. "It was an accident," he says. "I told Zeke I didn't mean to break the car, and I said I was sorry. Mom did not say anything about getting Zeke a new toy. I thought it was all over. Then Dad came home and insisted that I replace Zeke's car with my own money. I didn't mind that too much because it really was fair. But Mom said one thing and Dad said something different. They were changing the rules on me. I didn't like that."

"As the kids get older," Sam says, "they're going to become more and more tuned in to the points on which Kathy and I disagree, and those are the areas in which they're going to test us. We're going to have to stay aware of that."

Keith and Sari Grayson

"Once kids reach fourth grade," says Keith, "you pretty much lose control of them. They get into sports and school and afterschool activities. You really don't have much control after that."

"They do get awfully busy," says Sari, "but I wouldn't say you lose control. We still decide what activities they'll participate in. We never let them get involved in activities or groups that we don't approve of. We're pretty clear about expressing our values to the kids."

Twelve-year-old Charles is active in several groups outside school. "I play soccer in the fall, softball in the spring, and basketball whenever I can. I also belong to a model airplane club, and I have a collection of old comic books, especially World War II issues." He pauses, then grins and holds up his left arm, currently in a cast. "And I skateboard."

Charles's friends are a varied group. "My sports buddies all know one another," he explains, "but they don't know the guys in the airplane club, because they're interested in different things. The guys I skateboard with are surfer types, and they keep to themselves. I guess you could say I have different groups of friends."

His parents agree. "The kids Charles brings home are basically nice kids," says Sari, "but they are very different. He has friends from various social and ethnic groups."

"Charles chooses his friends on the basis of shared interests," says Keith. "If he enjoys doing something, he finds other people who enjoy doing the same thing. I'm pleased that factors like race and religion don't determine his choice of friends."

"My friends and I don't talk about religion," says Charles, "although I do know that some of them are half-Jewish, like me."

What does being half-Jewish mean to Charles? "I guess it means that one of your parents is Jewish, and so you go to a synagogue once in a while and celebrate a couple of Jewish holidays."

Charles thinks for a minute. "You know, being half-and-half is usually no big deal, but sometimes it's sort of awkward, like the time at my parents' anniversary party, when I was ten. Both of my grandmas were there. Grandma Sadie, the Jewish one, asked if I was going to have a bar mitzvah, and Grandma Lucy was standing right there! I knew that no matter what I said, one of them was going to get her feelings hurt. So I said that I didn't know yet."

Charles is not going to have a bar mitzvah. "The main reason," Keith explains, "is that he has no extra time to go to Hebrew school. There's just no way to work in one more activity. If he went to Hebrew school, he'd have to cut back on something else. Besides, he never brought up the subject."

"No, he never did," Sari says, "and we always assumed that if the kids were interested in having a bat or bar mitzvah, they'd ask us about it."

"I think that having a bar or bat mitzvah would be an overstatement," Keith says. "I mean, we agreed to expose the kids to both religions, not to raise them in one or the other. Having a bar or bat mitzvah would be a clear statement that they're Jewish, which they're not."

"A few of my cousins and friends have had a bar or bat mitzvah," says Charles. "Having a bar mitzvah is pretty neat, in a way. It's true that the kid is always nervous, and it's probably kind of embarrassing to have your grandparents and your old relatives get all emotional. But the bar mitzvah kid always seems to have a real good time at the party afterward, and everybody gives him money for college and presents. I don't know—if most of my friends were having a bar mitzvah or if my parents wanted me to, I might have one. But my mom and dad never brought up the idea."

Keith and Sari share a nondirective approach to parenting. "You don't have to do a lot of teaching and preaching," says Keith. "Kids learn basically by example, especially when it comes to morality. You just have to behave ethically, and kids will follow your example."

"Morality is kind of a personal thing," Charles says. "I mean, I can't tell you what I actually believe. To an extent, you have to make up your own mind about what's right and wrong. Like lying is wrong. Everyone knows that. But what if telling the truth would get someone in trouble? It's also wrong to get people in trouble. But what if they deserve to get into trouble because they really did something wrong? It's a personal thing, and the right answer isn't always the obvious one."

Charles hesitates, then continues. "Once I was at a hobby shop with a friend of mine, who was buying some parts for a model airplane. The guy at the cash register gave my friend too much change, ten dollars too much. My friend was really happy and considered going back in and spending the money, but then he thought that maybe the clerk would realize what happened, so he didn't go back in. I didn't say anything. Maybe he should have given it back, but the mistake wasn't his fault. He didn't cheat the guy. The guy made a mistake, and it just happened that my friend got the benefit. That's life."

What would Charles have done if he had gotten the extra change? "I don't know. Maybe I would've given it back, but not giving it back wasn't really wrong."

How does Charles decide what is right? "Sometimes I ask my friends, but mostly I just think about a situation until I decide what to do. And sometimes I talk to my parents, depending on what it's about."

Charles was asked what he thinks are the differences between Christianity and Judaism. "Well, the only differences I've seen between Judaism and Christianity are the holidays and the fact that Christians believe in Jesus and Jews don't. Both religions believe in God and teach you to be good to other people. I don't really think they're all that different."

Hannah, now in her mid-teens, recalls her elementary school years. "At first, being Jewish and Christian was really fun," she says. "Then, it started feeling strange, kind of awkward. All the other kids who celebrated Chanukah observed lots of Jewish holidays, but our family only celebrated Chanukah. I felt that celebrating Chanukah didn't make us even half-Jewish."

Hannah's mother remembers when her daughter reached that point. "Hannah started asking all sorts of questions about what religion we *really* were," Sari says. "It seemed as though she wanted us to choose one religion over the other instead of celebrating both. I told her that I thought it was an advantage to have two religions, that you could understand two points of view and two ways of thinking about life, but she didn't see it that way. In fact, she still doesn't see it that way."

"When she was about nine or ten, she started asking some tough questions," says Keith, "like why God lets bad things happen. To be honest, I didn't know enough theology to answer them. What I tried to do was to get her to do some reading and thinking and come up with her own answers. I didn't want to get into theology or imply that I had all the answers."

"We tried to keep our comments open-ended," says Sari. "We didn't want to give her the impression that there was just one right answer."

In a later conversation without her parents present, Hannah responded to their comments. "I realized at that point that my parents didn't really want us to be any religion. They wanted to celebrate the holidays without making a religious commitment. They wouldn't even answer questions about God. They just kept saying, 'Well, what do *you* think?' But I didn't know what to think! No one had ever told me what either religion was about. So how could I know what I thought?"

In response to Hannah's interest, Sari decided to practice more Judaism in the home. "That year, we made latkes and played the dreidel game. I taught the kids a couple of Chanukah songs, and I made sure we lit the menorah all eight nights. We also had a big party on the last day. The kids liked it a lot, but Keith was a little put out. He said something like, 'Hey, that's not fair. You get eight nights, and Christmas is only one day.' It was a joke, of course, but I think he was somewhat serious. Because his feelings were a little hurt, I now do less during Chanukah."

"The problem with just celebrating the holidays is that you never really learn much about the religion," says Hannah. "When I was about ten, I wanted to go to Hebrew school to learn about the Jewish faith. But I knew I'd get a lot of static, so I didn't ask. I wish my parents would have taken me more seriously and answered my questions. At least then, we would have talked about religion."

Charles is more accepting of his parents' decision. "Being half-and-half is no big deal," he says. "It doesn't really matter."

Comments

Whether religion is important to a school-aged child or not depends primarily on how important it is to his parents.

Sam and Kathy want their children to adopt Jewish values and viewpoints. The Cohens encourage their boys to question and explore religious ideas. Danny has assimilated the Jewish principles that he has learned both at home and in Hebrew school. He feels comfortable expressing his viewpoint, even when it differs from that of his parents. For instance, he wore his yarmulka at meals for several weeks, despite the fact that the practice was not shared by his father.

Sam and Kathy make a concerted effort to give Danny a connection with Jewish children through the temple and Jewish camps. They have successfully conveyed the message to

Danny that he is a Jew, despite his mother's non-Jewish background. From Danny's perspective, being half-Jewish and half-Christian is incomprehensible. He sums up his opinion: "You can't half believe in Jesus and half not believe."

On the other hand, Keith and Sari tell their children that they are half-and-half. For Charles, it's "no big deal." Like many children in his situation, he gives the following functional definition of being half-and-half: "I guess it means that one of your parents is Jewish, and so you go to a synagogue once in a while and celebrate a couple of Jewish holidays." Asked to be more specific, he answers, "I can't tell you what I actually believe." Asked to compare Christianity and Judaism, he responds, "I don't really think they're all that different." Keith and Sari have succeeded in minimizing the differences between the two faiths.

Yet there are times when being half-and-half makes Charles uncomfortable. He resents having been put in the no-win situation wherein no matter what he said about having a bar mitzvah celebration, one of his grandmothers "was going to get her feelings hurt." He is also ambivalent about whether to have a bar mitzvah. He says that if he felt his peers or parents expected him to go through that experience, he might do it, but his parents never initiated a conversation about his having a bar mitzvah.

While Charles waited for his parents' guidance concerning this issue, they waited to see if he would bring it up. Sari asserts that "if the kids were interested in a bar or bat mitzvah, they'd ask us about it." Keith says that while he wants to expose the children to both religions, "having a bar mitzvah would be an overstatement."

Sari and Keith also point out that Charles is too busy for Hebrew school, maintaining that "there's just no way to work in one more activity." In contrast, Sam and Kathy view the time they spend on Danny's Jewish education comparable to that given by other parents to "soccer or music lessons or ice skating or gymnastics or something else for their kids." Both couples are, in fact, willing to devote considerable time and energy to activities for their children's growth and development, but their respective values determine which activities they choose.

Keith and Sari have adopted the philosophy that "you just have to behave ethically, and kids will follow your example." Yet Charles was ambivalent when his friend kept money that did not belong to him, saying that "it wasn't really wrong." If he had been given a specific ethical perspective, he might have been able to determine what was "right."

While Charles seems comfortable with his parents' approach to religion, Hannah is less satisfied. When she was in elementary school, she concluded that "celebrating Chanukah didn't make us even half-Jewish," and she started asking questions about religion. In their attempt to give "open-ended" answers, Keith and Sari provided her with little information and less guidance. They expected her to research her questions and form her own judgments instead of relying on her parents for answers. But Hannah was a child, looking for information and direction, not permission to make her own decisions about religion. Looking back, Hannah says, "No one ever told me what either religion was about. So how could I know what I thought?" She still wishes her parents had answered her questions directly. "At least then we would have talked about religion," she says. Hannah was so sure that her parents would not support her idea of going to Hebrew school that she did not even bring it up.

While Keith and Sari convey to their children the explicit message that they are half-Christian and half-Jewish, their implicit message is that neither religion is important. As Charles says, "Being half-and-half is no big deal. It doesn't really matter."

For the child of intermarriage, middle childhood is a watershed. He starts to ask difficult questions and wants clear answers, even if he chooses to disregard them. If his parents answer his serious questions lightly or respond to complex issues with ambiguous answers, the child becomes discouraged or frustrated. If his questions bring him no new information, he will probably stop asking them. Conversely, if the answers he receives are engaging, his questioning will continue. He will consider, adopt, reject, and reconsider ideas based on his level of intellectual and emotional readiness.

As the child moves through the elementary years into adolescence, his focus will continue to shift away from the family, and he will begin to make decisions that prepare him for life on his own.

✦ ✦ ✦ ───────────────────────────────

Chapter 6

Adolescence and the Teen Years

- Is having a religious identity important to the adolescent?
- Are the teen years more difficult for the children of intermarriage than for the children of same-faith couples?
- How do teenage children of intermarriage deal with ethical dilemmas?

Introduction

Adolescence is a time for making choices. The teenager becomes aware of career and lifestyle options. She explores the limits of her own decision-making and risk-taking abilities. She realizes that she is free to accept or reject her parents' values. In short, the adolescent is in the process of defining her place in the world.

Like all teens, children of intermarriage grapple with the issue of their religious identity. Their responses to religion are as individual as the children themselves are. Teenagers raised in one parent's religion tend to identify themselves as being of that faith, but sometimes they include a reference to the other faith. "I'm Christian with Jewish overtones" and "I'm a Jew with Christian relatives" are typical comments. Children raised in a family that observes both Christian and Jewish traditions church youth group through high school. It wasn't the central thing in my life, but it was where I could go to talk about what was important to me. It also reinforced the values I had been taught at home, and that extra support helped me."

"I pretty much stopped going to temple after my bar mitzvah," says Sam, "but I never stopped thinking of myself as Jewish. As long as I lived at home, I always went to High Holiday services. But after all those years of Hebrew school, I thought I deserved some time off."

"Well, I hope our kids find a different way to assert their independence," Kathy says. "There are so many pressures on kids these days that I think it would help them if they stayed connected with the temple."

"Maybe," says Sam. "But if they're like me, they may stop going to temple when they're thirteen or fourteen. However, they'll always know they're Jewish."

What would Sam's and Kathy's reaction be if their children rejected Judaism? "Frankly, I'd be deeply disappointed," says Sam. "But if they decide on something else or if they decide not to have any religious affiliation, that's their decision."

"To me," says Kathy, "religion is a very personal thing. We're doing everything we can now to make sure that the boys develop a love for the rituals and principles of Judaism. If they leave it behind later, at least they'll have some basis for making an adult-level decision. They'll know what they're rejecting."

"I think that kids sometimes reject their religion, whatever it is, just because it's their parents' thing," says Sam. "But I think that when a kid rejects his parents' ideas, it's often temporary. Remember what Mark Twain said? Something to the effect that when he was fourteen, he was surprised at how little his father knew, and then when he was twenty-one, he was amazed at how much his father had learned in seven years. It may take time, but often kids come to accept their parents' ideas."

The Cohens regard the bar mitzvah experience as an important part of adolescence. "Studying for his bar mitzvah gives a kid something to concentrate on, a goal to work toward," says Kathy. "It's up to the kid to make of it what he wants. No one but the bar mitzvah can take credit for his work. If he does a good job, he can take all the glory; if he blows it, he can't blame anyone but himself. I think that it challenges a kid to work hard and do well. And most kids do."

"I've known some kids who had doubts about having a bar mitzvah," says Sam. "For instance, I had a nephew who told his parents after four years of Hebrew school that he wasn't going to go through with the ceremony because he wasn't sure he believed in God. His parents replied that he didn't have to have a bar mitzvah unless he wanted one, but they asked him to think about the bar mitzvah as a cultural event, as a way of identifying himself as a member of the Jewish people. I want the bar mitzvah of both our boys to be not only a religious statement but also an affirmation of their identification with their Jewish heritage."

"We've been to some very fancy bar mitzvah parties," Kathy says. "They seemed too elaborate for thirteen-year-old kids and completely unrelated to the idea behind becoming a bar mitzvah. I think that the bar mitzvah experience should reflect Jewish culture, not resemble a Hawaiian luau or a Tex-Mex fiesta.

"I know that there's a countermovement right now against lavish bar mitzvah parties," Kathy continues. "Some families are planning very modest parties and donating the rest of what they might have spent to charity. And some children are asking their parents to save for their college education rather than spend money on a fancy party. The emphasis is on the ceremony in the temple, where the kid reads the Torah portion and the parents pass the Torah to him, and so on. I think that it's a healthy shift."

"I've been to many bar and bat mitzvahs," says Danny. "Some were really neat, but some were not so good. At one, the kid was pulled into the party room in a rickshaw. I didn't get it. I mean, the kid wasn't Japanese or anything."

"The best bar mitzvah I ever went to was my cousin Jacob's," says Zeke. "It was in a beautiful synagogue, they had these big baskets of candies, and everyone took some candy and threw it at Jake after he read the Torah. They had lunch afterward with bagels and potato salad and a gigantic cake. It was neat. I want mine to be like that."

"I want mine to be like Ethan's was—he's this friend of ours," says Danny. "He included some of his friends in the actual service, and then the party was on the patio of the synagogue. They had an old-time Jewish band and Jewish food like knishes and bagels. It was a lot of fun."

What does becoming a bar mitzvah mean to Danny and Zeke? "It means you're a grown-up," says Zeke.

"It's an accomplishment," says Dan, "because you have to work hard to learn your Torah portion. And you can feel proud of carrying on a tradition that goes back thousands of years."

Keith and Sari Grayson

"If you asked me about being a teenager in general," says Keith, "I'd say it was a lot of fun. There was a feeling of being free without having a lot of responsibility. You could do pretty much what you wanted, and you didn't have to earn a living."

What significance did religion have to Keith and Sari when they were teenagers?

"What I remember most about my teenage years is that the church we attended was basically a social center," Keith says. "The kids in the youth group weren't particularly religious. We didn't go around talking about being 'saved' or anything like that. We had volleyball and softball leagues and parties. We hardly ever went to church services."

"I stayed involved in Jewish youth groups right up until college," says Sari. "In high school, most of my friends were the kids from the temple and the Jewish Community Center. It wasn't a big religious thing. We weren't superobservant, but we did talk about morality and ethics and we got involved in social action. We also goofed off and had fun. In a way, I'm sorry our kids haven't been part of a similar peer group."

"I don't think the kids are missing anything," says Keith. "After all, the most important part of church for a teenager is the social aspect, and our kids have very active social lives."

"It wasn't just the kids that made the youth groups special for me," says Sari, "it was also the advisers. Having adults other than my parents to talk to was an important part of belonging to the teen groups. You can't tell your parents everything, no matter how close you are."

"I think all teenagers have problems from time to time with their parents," says Keith. "I know that I drove my folks crazy. I stayed out late and didn't tell them where I was going, and I hung around with kids they didn't like. And for eight straight years, they begged me to get a haircut. But that's part of growing up."

Keith feels that he had been only mildly defiant as a teenager. "My parents didn't make a bunch of unreasonable demands," says Keith. "In general, the rules in our family weren't too strict, and when I broke them, it was usually because the fun I was having was worth the consequence."

"I didn't do anything rebellious until I married Keith," says Sari. "That was probably enough of a rebellion for one lifetime."

"I think we're doing pretty well with our kids," says Keith. "We got Hannah through puberty and into her teen years, and Charles is making it through adolescence okay."

"I find that the hardest part about adolescence for me as a parent is the mood swings," says Sari. "For the whole year that Hannah was thirteen, she was on a roller-coaster ride. One minute she was fine; the next she was a wreck. She burst into tears at least once a day, and you never knew what was going to set her off. It was a nightmare. But she, and we, got through it."

"Can you imagine what it would have been like if she had also had a bat mitzvah that year?" Keith asks. "I shudder to think about it."

"I don't know about that," Sari says. "I remember my bat mitzvah as one of the best days of my life. Everyone was there to honor *me*. They came to see *me*, to hear *me* read the Torah. It was a great feeling. My bat mitzvah did a lot to get me through the insecurities of that time of life. Maybe Hannah could have used an experience like that at thirteen."

"But you're Jewish," says Keith, "and Hannah's not. It wouldn't have meant the same to her. Remember, she never asked to have a bat mitzvah. And none of the kids ever asked to be confirmed in a church or baptized, either. I don't think they're missing anything."

"I know my Jewish grandma wanted me to have a bar mitzvah," says Charles. "She said she'd make the party and everything if I'd go to Hebrew school. But I didn't do it. In a way I wanted to. All the bar mitzvahs I've been to were pretty neat. But it didn't seem right because I'm not really Jewish. My grandma said that since my mom's Jewish, Heather, Hannah, and I are all Jewish, and so I could have a bar mitzvah if I wanted one. But I don't feel Jewish, and my parents never brought up the idea."

"I know my mother has spoken to the kids about having bar and bat mitzvahs," says Sari. "I feel that she's cheating, going around me and talking directly to them about it. At the same time, part of me wishes they had said yes."

Charles says, "All of the guys who had bar mitzvahs complained about going to Hebrew school because they missed out on other stuff. But they're usually glad they did it. Some of my friends who have one Jewish parent celebrated their bar mitzvahs and invited their Christian relatives. If I were going to have a bar mitzvah, I don't know how I would feel about my Christian grandma's being there. I think I'd feel uncomfortable."

He continues, "I remember that at my cousin's bar mitzvah, I was sitting next to my aunt and uncle, watching how proud they looked. And for a minute I thought, Boy, I'd like my parents to look at me that way."

What are sixteen-year-old Hannah's views on Jewish and Christian values? "You know, my parents are really proud that they raised us both religions," she says. "But I don't buy it. Even though some of my friends who are half-and-half really like it, I don't. We have extra holidays but nothing else. It seems to me that a religion should help you deal with difficult situations, but I never got any consistent Jewish or Christian information on morality or anything like that. I think that if my parents had been serious about religion, my mom would have told us about Jewish ideas and my dad would have explained Christian ideas. Then we could have made up our own mind."

How would Hannah describe her religious identity? "Nothing," she says promptly. "I'm not both. I'm nothing." She points out that religion is not like race: It is not biological. "It's not like having a Japanese mother and an Eskimo father, so you're half-Japanese and half-Eskimo."

Hannah and her parents have talked about her views. "Yes, I know Hannah has her own feelings about the way we've done things," Sari says. "What teenager doesn't? When I was her age, I complained about the things that my parents did. But Hannah has to understand that we're doing the best we can. It wouldn't have been fair for us to decide which religion our children should follow. We each had to consider the feelings of the other parent. Hannah doesn't understand all the aspects involved. If she had wanted a bat mitzvah, she could have studied and had one."

"Or she could take a confirmation class and be confirmed in the church," says Keith. "It's entirely up to her, and so far she's chosen neither option."

Hannah may follow up on one of those options. "I'm thinking about it," she says. "I might join a church or a synagogue, if it felt right. But the problem would be my parents. How would my dad feel if I joined a synagogue? What would my mom say if I were baptized and became a Christian? I think one of them would be very hurt. It would be like choosing one over the other. I know that when they decided that we would be a half-Christian, half-Jewish family, they were trying to be fair. But they were only being fair to themselves, not to us."

"If it's important enough to her, she'll do something," says Sari. "Maybe not right away, maybe not until she's in college, but eventually she'll do what's important to her."

"I wish I had a religion that I grew up with," Hannah says. "I'd like to have a religion that is like a hometown—something you can think about and remember and know it's yours. Even if you moved to another town, you would still have your hometown with you, in a way. All the memories of growing up there would still be a part of you. That's what I think it would be like to have a religion. Even if I didn't practice it or I moved away from it, it would still be mine. I feel as though I don't know where I'm from."

Comments

Both couples recognize the importance of respecting a teen-ager's growing independence. They realize that a teenager's focus is outside the family and that her friends are the most important people in her life. Both couples think back to the highs and lows of their own teen years to help them guide their adolescent children.

The Cohens have what might be regarded as traditional ex-pectations for their children's religious involvement. They have planned the sequence of Jewish life-cycle events that began with Danny's *berit* and are making certain that their sons get a Jewish education. Danny and Zeke look forward to becoming bar mitzvahs as a natural part of growing up. Sam and Kathy accept the fact that their sons may complain about attending Hebrew school, but they do not give the boys the option of dropping out.

The Cohens have found support as an interfaith family within the Jewish community. Their temple, which has developed policies responsive to the needs of intermarried couples who want to raise Jewish children, does not differentiate between children who have one Jewish parent and those who have two Jewish parents.

More than Sam, Kathy feels that it is important for the boys to continue being members of a temple through their teen years. Kathy sees the temple as a potential source of emotional and moral support for the boys. For Sam, being Jewish is a matter of culture as much as religion. He accepts the possibility that Dan and Zeke might leave the temple when they become teen-agers. He notes that he maintained his Jewish identity throughout his teen and early-adult years without practicing Jewish rituals or belonging to a synagogue.

Both Sam and Kathy acknowledge that they would be very disappointed if either of their sons abandoned Judaism. But they recognize that religious affiliation is a personal choice.

The Graysons have provided their children with good role models, a variety of holidays, and few specifics about ethics and religion. Keith and Sari trust that their children will grow up to be open-minded and ethical because they were raised in a family that observed the holidays of both parents' religions and stressed moral behavior.

Hannah finds her parents' plan lacking. She complains that in their attempt to celebrate both sets of religious holidays without emphasizing either, her parents may have created a win-win situation for themselves but a losing one for their children. Hannah wants more than holiday celebrations from religion. Her complaint that she "never got any consistent Jewish or Christian information on morality" contradicts Keith's repeated assertion that he doesn't think his children "are missing anything."

Keith and Sari reassure each other that their children will ask questions if they become interested in religion. But Hannah hesitates to explore one parent's faith for fear of hurting the other parent's feelings, and Charles says that his parents "never mentioned" his having a bar mitzvah.

The Grayson family's solution illustrates what often happens in dual-religion families. The parents believe that they have made available to their children the best of Judaism and Christianity, while the children feel alienated from both faiths. Hannah's equating not having a religion with not having a hometown underscores her desire for roots.

◆ ◆ ◆

Chapter 7

The Empty Nest—
After the Children Leave Home

- How does life change for an interfaith couple after their children leave home?
- Do an interfaith couple's child-rearing choices affect their life as a couple after their children leave home?
- What role does an interfaith couple expect to play in their children's ritual life once the children have left home?

Introduction

A new phase of family life begins after the children leave home. Sociologists have identified this empty-nest stage as a time of potential stress for parents. A woman whose career has been child rearing may have a surplus of time and energy once her children leave. Some parents experience depression and loneliness when their children move out. But this stage also creates an opportunity for a couple to reclaim and renew their relationship.

Just as a couple constituted a family before their children were born, they are a family of two once again after their children leave. Ideally, a couple will be able to use this period to become reacquainted with each other. Empty nesters often find themselves reinstituting old routines or developing new habits that border on the self-indulgent, pampering themselves as they could not when their children lived with them.

Family rituals may also change for couples whose children have left home. Some couples no longer find it necessary to observe those traditions that helped them give their children a culture or a value system. After their children have launched lives of their own, parents may continue or discard practices as they wish, adopting new routines or reestablishing rituals they had enjoyed at the beginning of their relationship.

One of the pleasant surprises often mentioned by empty-nest couples is their grown children's eagerness to return home for holidays and other family occasions. Young adults, even ones who only a few short years before had fought protracted battles with their parents over participation in family events, often insist on continuing family traditions. The home of many parents remains the focus for family gatherings, the place where adult children bring their own children to share the family's customs and heritage.

Adult children often enjoy reliving childhood traditions in their parents' home and introducing their spouses and children to the rituals they cherish. New ways of celebrating family events are often invented by grandparents and their grandchildren. These rituals may replace, even if they do not duplicate, the ones the grandparents practiced with their own children.

When interfaith couples reach the empty-nest phase, they may discover that the religious practices they had chosen to follow when their children were small now seem inappropriate. They may discard holidays or rituals they had been observing "for the children's sake" and resume those they practiced as a couple before the children were born. If they had joined a church or synagogue for the sole purpose of providing their children with a religious education, they are now likely to discontinue their membership.

Couples may assume that their actions have no impact on their absent children. But changes in their parents' lifestyle are often surprisingly significant to grown children, who may complain when their parents abandon a family ritual. "You always said that was important," they may protest. "You always made us do it, and now you don't do it yourselves." The logical, if unspoken, conclusion is, Maybe it was never important at all. Young adults will often drop a practice that their parents worked for years to instill in them simply because their parents have decided to abandon it.

Sam and Kathy Cohen

"It's funny," says Kathy, "that with all the talking we've done about different aspects of family life, we hadn't talked much about what will happen after the kids leave home. Then last summer, when Danny was at camp and Zeke was spending a few days with Sam's parents, we were home alone, and we suddenly realized, Hey, this is what it'll be like when the kids go off to college. It wasn't bad."

"Not bad?" Sam says. "It was great! We could eat whenever we wanted, go to a movie if we felt like it, make love with the bedroom door open, sleep in on the weekends. Our life was our own. But we knew it was only going to be for a few days. It will be different when they leave for good."

How will the Cohens handle holiday celebrations after the boys leave home? "Well, I know Sam is not comfortable with the idea of celebrating Christian holidays," says Kathy, "and I don't think he ever will be. We dealt with that before we got married, so I don't expect to start having a Christmas tree just because the boys are gone. I'm quite sure we'll go on celebrating Jewish holidays."

"I think it's very important to continue celebrating Jewish holidays in our home," says Sam. "When Dan and Zeke go to college, we expect them to come home during vacations, and I think they should find things as familiar as possible. Then, after they're on their own, married or whatever, their roots will still be here, and there will be something here for them and their children to come back to."

How does Kathy feel about continuing her active involvement in Jewish traditions and rituals? "Actually," says Kathy,

"I never thought about it until last summer when the kids were both gone. It occurred to me then that when the kids move out, I might like to start going to church again. I mentioned that to Sam, and for the first time we talked about what will happen when the kids are gone. It ended up being a heavy discussion."

"I have mixed feelings about Kathy's reaffiliating with her church," says Sam. "Not that I object to her going to Christian services. In theory, I don't. Her religion is her business. It's just that the boys have always known her to be active in the temple. To them, she's essentially a Jewish mother. I don't know what message would be conveyed if she suddenly stopped her activities at the temple and started going to church."

Do Sam and Kathy think that their children will come home for Jewish holidays and rituals? "We have friends whose kids are already in college or living on their own," says Kathy. "It seems as though kids go through a period of not wanting to come home for anything—not for holidays, not for vacations, not for anything. I don't think they're rejecting religious traditions as much as expressing their independence, because some of them make a point of attending Christmas Eve services or going to a seder wherever they are. And after they've exercised their independence for a year or two, many of them seem ready to reestablish contact. I remember going through something like that, so I think we'd better be prepared."

"We've also seen parents who discontinued holiday celebrations because their kids had stopped coming home," says Sam. "When the kids started coming back, they felt that something was missing."

"We have plenty of friends and relatives to celebrate with if the kids decide not to come home for the holidays," says Kathy. "We could always celebrate holidays with people from the temple and, of course, Sam's family. When and if the boys decide to come home again for the holidays, they could just join us."

"I think they should have a Jewish family to come back to," Sam says. "That's why I worry about your going to church again."

"I don't know what I'll do," says Kathy. "On the one hand,

it seems to me that once the boys have established their Jewish identities and are out in the world, it shouldn't matter to them what I do. I've always been honest with Dan and Zeke about the fact that I'm not Jewish. I don't know if it would confuse or disturb them if I started going to church. On the other hand, Sam's right. I've always participated fully in Jewish holidays and in the temple, so maybe it wouldn't be such a good idea. I guess Sam and I need to talk about this. We also need to get the boys' reactions. Also, lately I've started thinking that someday the boys will probably expect me to be a Jewish grandmother to their children. That's kind of unnerving."

"And the question is," Sam interjects, "does a Jewish grandmother go to church? Whether or not Danny and Zeke marry Jewish women, I think they'll want their kids to have Jewish experiences. At least, I hope they will. We may be the only Jewish grandparents our grandchildren will have. We've got to provide a Jewish experience for them. And since, statistically at least, Kathy will probably outlive me, she may well be the only Jewish grandparent those children will have."

"When I realized that, I was slightly stunned," Kathy recalls. "I had never thought our situation through that far. I think that if we're going to end up being Jewish grandparents, we should stay involved in the temple, even after the kids have left home."

Sam looks at her in surprise.

"Well, if we're going to provide a Jewish home base for our kids and grandchildren," Kathy says, "I want us to be part of the Jewish community. To me, practicing a religion isn't something that you do temporarily, just to indoctrinate the children. Religion isn't something you can put on and take off like a coat, according to the season. If we are in fact a Jewish family, we've got to be a Jewish family for keeps, and to me that includes belonging to the temple."

"I have mixed feelings about belonging to the temple after the boys leave home," says Sam. "I mean, we joined primarily for the kids. I didn't think there'd be much of anything for me there. But I admit I've become more involved than I ever thought I would be. Being part of a temple again brings back lots of really nice feelings and memories from my childhood. I'm also enjoying watching Dan and Zeke learn about our history and get a sense of their Judaism. But I'm not sure about belonging to the temple after the kids leave home. I'd rather not commit to that just yet."

Kathy smiles. "That's more of a commitment than I've ever heard Sam make. But you know, I've changed, too. Ten years ago, I participated in Jewish traditions more as a guest than anything else. But I've become genuinely involved. My year revolves around the Jewish calendar now. The High Holy Days and Passover are the holidays for which I plan, cook, and buy the kids new clothes. While I don't see myself converting to Judaism, I've certainly become more than a passive bystander. I feel that I'm definitely part of the Jewish community and a member of a Jewish family."

"So we've both changed," says Sam. "And when the kids leave home, things will continue to change."

"When I go to college," Danny predicts, "I'll still do all the Jewish things, like go to a seder. I went to one at a college once, so I know they have them there. Or I might come home. Or I might go to Nana and Papa's house. Then, when I get married, Mom and Dad will be the grandparents, and they'll have Jewish holidays here. That's what grandparents do."

Does Dan think that his parents will continue to belong to the temple after he and Zeke move away? "Why not?" he asks. "My parents do lots of stuff there that's just for grown-ups, like go to lectures and fund-raisers. They'll probably do that forever."

Keith and Sari Grayson

"When you have three kids," says Keith, "and they're as active as ours are, you know things will change when they leave home. No more sports, Scouts, clubs, school plays, gymnastics. No more car pools, no more gangs of kids around all the time, no more phone ringing off the hook. You bet it'll be different!"

"I dread it, in a way," says Sari. "I'm always the one driving on the field trips, manning the bake-sale booths, making soccer banners and costumes for the plays, and arranging car pools all over town. It's been a full-time job for the past sixteen years, and I see it going on for ten more, until Heather graduates from high school."

Sari has not worked outside the house since Hannah was born. "It's not that we don't need the money," says Keith. "Heaven knows, we could use it. But we decided that Sari would stay home and be involved in the kids' activities. As a result, the kids have been able to do lots of things they couldn't have done if she had been working."

"Being the superparent has been my job," says Sari. "And I love it. But it's a job with a forced retirement date. I guess I should prepare myself for something else before that time comes. I'd hate to wake up one morning and have absolutely nothing to do!"

"Sari's life will change much more than mine will after the kids leave home," Keith points out. "I'll still go to work and wash the car on the weekend. She's going to have to find other things to do."

"I'm not going to be one of those displaced homemakers," says Sari. "I'll find lots of things to be involved in. Besides, the kids won't fall off the end of the earth. They'll be around. We'll still have holidays together and birthdays and other special times."

Do Keith and Sari expect the children to return home for holiday celebrations? "I don't see why not," Keith says. "We've always had Christmas and Easter and Chanukah together."

"Ours has always been the house in which everyone congregates," Sari says. "Hannah and Charles always have their friends over here. Even now, I never know how many there will be for dinner. I envision lots of family and friends around for holidays."

"Kids always have school vacations," Keith says, "even in college. I expect they'll bring their friends home for Christmas and Easter, and it will be pretty much like it is now, only the kids will be bigger. And eventually they'll bring their own children."

Will the family's holiday traditions change? "We have a miniature Christmas town that we put under the tree and that we add to every year," says Keith. "It will keep expanding, and eventually our grandchildren, when they come along, will have favorite pieces that they will add. And Sari will teach Hannah and Heather and Charles's wife how to make the Christmas cookies."

"Wait a minute," Sari interjects. "I'm going to teach Charles, and he can teach his wife!"

"The point is," Keith continues, "that the traditions will continue and be passed on to the next generation, no matter who does the passing."

"I'm sure that my mother will make the first seder forever, even if she has to serve the matzah-ball soup from her deathbed," Sari predicts. "My sister and I usually take turns making the second seder. However, I don't know if I'd go to all that trouble if the kids weren't coming. We might just go to my mom's the first night and leave it at that. Because Chanukah is basically a little kids' holiday, there will probably be a period after our kids get too big—but before we have grandchildren—when we won't celebrate it."

Hannah will be off to college in just two years. "I'd like to live on campus," she says. "It's not that I'm anxious to get away from home. It's just that I think living in a dorm is a big part of the college experience, and my parents agree. Of course, I'll come home for Christmas. I wouldn't miss it. I don't know about Chanukah. It depends on when it is, finals, and other things. I'm not so sure about Easter, either. I'd like to go to the beach during Easter break. That's sort of traditional, isn't it? As for Passover—if I can get away for Grandma Sadie's seder, I definitely will. It'll depend on how far away I am and which college I attend.

"But I worry about Mom," Hannah continues. "Her feelings might be hurt if we didn't come home for all the holidays. They mean a lot to her."

Charles has not given much thought to living away from home. "I don't know," he says. "Holidays are different when you're not a kid anymore. Last Christmas, I just wasn't into it until about two days before the holiday. The whole thing seemed corny and absurd. Then suddenly, on about the twenty-third, I just got the Christmas spirit I guess, and I went shopping in a big rush. I don't know what's going to happen this year, and I have no idea what it will be like when I'm in college. Maybe I won't want to come home at all. Even though celebrating the holidays is a big deal to Mom and Dad, I just don't know what I'll do."

Comments

It is difficult for young couples to visualize the future and imagine their life after their children move away. Many couples return to some of the practices and habits they had as a twosome before their children were born. Most couples modify traditions to accommodate their grown children and others in their extended family.

The Cohens and Graysons feel well equipped to weather the stressful empty-nest period. Both couples are aware of the importance of maintaining a close relationship and open communication. Both couples state that they share interests besides the children and that they look forward to being alone together again. However, until they were asked to think specifically about how they think their life will change after their children leave home, both couples admitted that they had given the matter little thought.

For Sam and Kathy, the issue of which holidays to celebrate and which rituals to continue after the boys leave home is a thorny one. Kathy had put aside her own religious celebrations in order to create a Jewish family life, with the original thought that she might someday rejoin a church. Now she is beginning to think about the importance of providing a Jewish home base for Dan and Zeke when they are grown and about her future role as the mother in a Jewish family. She is also beginning to acknowledge that Jewish holidays and traditions have taken on a special meaning for her personally. Although she is not considering conversion, Kathy, nonetheless, sees herself as a member of the Jewish community and finds the community's support an important part of her life. She and

Sam have just begun to talk about whether they will stay involved in the temple after the boys leave home.

Keith and Sari know that the pace of activity at their house will slow considerably after their children leave, but they do expect to see Hannah, Charles, and Heather on a regular basis. They assume that their children will want to come home for Christmas and Easter. Because Sari sees Chanukah as a "little kids' holiday," she plans to ignore it once her children are out of the house until the time that her grandchildren arrive on the scene. Also, she doubts she'll put in the effort of preparing a seder if the children do not come home. At this point, Keith and Sari do not feel that they will observe many holiday and life-cycle events after their children leave home. They expect to observe only two or three holiday traditions as a couple, none of which is associated with Chanukah or Passover.

Both couples have made life-style decisions based on what they thought would be in their children's best interests, and both of them have had to adjust their expectations. In particular, Kathy gave up her Christian involvement in order to give her children a Jewish family life. Now Kathy is beginning to think about if and when she might resume her own religious traditions.

In response to Kathy's statement that she might like to go back to her church after the boys leave home, Sam asks, "Does a Jewish grandmother go to church?" However, he is nonplussed when Kathy replies that Jewish grandparents should belong to the temple. It seems that his view of himself as a cultural Jew conflicts with Kathy's perception of their family as Jewishly observant. But both Sam and Kathy recognize how they have changed as individuals, as a couple, and as parents raising Jewish children and that there is no sure way of predicting where those changes will lead them in the future.

Questions and problems that are raised and created by intermarriage do not all arise at the beginning of a couple's relationship. An interfaith couple is likely to confront issues stemming from their religious differences throughout the child-rearing years and beyond.

Chapter **8**

◆ ◆ ◆ —————————————————————————

The Grandparent Connection

- How are interfaith families influenced by grand-parents?
- How do grandparents feel about their grandchildren born of an interfaith marriage?
- How do the children of intermarriage feel toward their grandparents?

Introduction

For the parents of intermarried couples, the birth of their first grandchild is sometimes a bittersweet experience. Like all grandparents, they see the grandchild as their link with the future. But many of them also feel that the future of their religious group is at risk. Although they welcome the child, they worry about how firmly rooted she will be in their heritage and whether she will carry on their cultural legacy.

Marriage between Christians and Jews used to be rare. Within the Jewish community, intermarriage has always been viewed as a threat to the survival of Judaism. In the not-so-distant past, many Jewish parents responded to a child's intermarriage by sitting *shivah,* a mourning ritual, for the errant Jewish son or daughter. (This tradition is still practiced by some Orthodox Jews.) Although a few Christian denominations oppose marriage outside the faith, intermarriage is not viewed as an·imminent threat by most Protestant churches.

Parents of both faiths tend to discourage intermarriage for cultural as well as religious reasons. Many Jewish parents worry that marrying outside the religion will result in assimilation and the eventual disappearance of the Jewish people. They argue that Jewish survival tomorrow needs Jewish children today, and that Jewish children need Jewish homes. For their part, Christian parents often fear that if their children intermarry, their grandchildren will grow up outside the mainstream of our Christian-oriented society. Many Christian grandparents worry that their unbaptized grandchildren will not enter into everlasting life in heaven. Both Jewish and Christian parents fear that their intermarried children, along with their grandchildren, will be social and religious pariahs, accepted by neither community.

Even parents who are tolerant of intermarriage are concerned about the stresses that it will exert on their children and grandchildren. "Marriage and raising kids is hard enough," one mother told her adult daughter. "Marrying out of your faith just makes it harder." Her sentiment is widely shared.

Sam and Kathy Cohen

Neither Sam's nor Kathy's parents were enthusiastic about their child's marriage. "My parents always made it clear, implicitly and explicitly, that they expected me to marry a Jew," says Sam. "They like Kathy, but they would have been much happier if she were Jewish. That's only natural, I suppose."

"We weren't surprised when Sam married a Gentile," says Sam's mother. "Of course, we'd have preferred that he marry a Jewish woman, but what were we going to do? We don't live in an age of arranged marriages, and young people are going to marry whomever they want."

"What were we supposed to do?" Sam's father asks. "Disown him? He's still our son, and his children are our grandchildren."

"What did surprise us," Sam's mother says, "was that he was so adamant about raising the boys as Jews."

"I don't think Sam had set foot in a synagogue since his bar mitzvah," says Sam's father. "Then, boom! He has kids, and suddenly being involved in the Jewish community is important to him. So now he's on the temple board, the kids go to religious school, the whole bit. You could've knocked me over with a feather!"

"We're delighted that Danny and Zeke are being raised as Jews," Sam's mother says. "It's such a pleasure to have them at our seder table, reciting the Four Questions, knowing the blessings, learning about our heritage. So many of our friends have grandchildren who know almost nothing about Jewish life and Jewish traditions. Even some of the children whose parents are both Jewish aren't getting any kind of Jewish education. It's very sad."

"In our day," says Sam's father, "it was taken for granted that Jewish children would go to Hebrew school. Nowadays, it seems to be out of fashion, or maybe it's too much of a hassle. But our grandsons are carrying on the tradition, and that's the way it should be."

"It came as a surprise to us that Kathy agreed to raise the children as Jews," Sam's mother says. "We had our doubts about her decision, but she never takes the boys to church or involves them in any Christian practices. Not like our niece, who agreed to raised the children as Jews and then had them baptized."

"A disaster," Sam's father comments.

"But," Sam's mother wonders aloud, "what if, God forbid, something happened to Sam and Kathy had to raise the boys on her own? How could she keep on practicing the Jewish traditions and managing the boys' Jewish education? Would she decide to introduce them to her faith?"

"Let's hope the situation never arises," says Sam's father.

Sam's parents are concerned about the way Jewish traditions are observed in Sam and Kathy's home. "They belong to the temple," says Sam's father, "but it's a Reform temple and not as observant as the Conservative *shul* where Sam received his

Jewish training. They don't keep the dietary laws, they drive on Shabbat, and they take other liberties. Still, Dan and Zeke say that they're Jewish and that they're going to have a bar mitzvah, so we're very grateful."

"And we are also grateful that Kathy's family doesn't seem to push their religion," Sam's mother says. "At least, I've never heard Sam say anything that leads me to believe that they are negative about the boys' being Jewish."

"My parents are just happy that our kids are Jewish," Sam says. "I think they've gotten over wishing that Kathy were Jewish, as long as the boys are. For my parents, the children represent the future of Judaism."

Dan and Zeke feel a strong tie with their Jewish grandparents, Nana and Papa. "We were at their house," says Zeke, "and Nana showed us pictures of Daddy's bar mitzvah. It wasn't fancy, but everyone looked really happy. And Nana said she wanted to dance at my bar mitzvah and at Dan's. I said okay."

"Nana's and Papa's parents came to America about ninety years ago," Danny explains. "They had to leave their country because it wasn't safe to be Jewish there anymore. Jews were being killed for no reason. When they came to New York and saw the Statue of Liberty, they knew that they were free. They knew that no one would bother them about being Jewish here. It's almost like a story in a book, except that it's about real people and they were my great-grandparents."

"By the time Danny was on the way," says Kathy, "my parents were used to the idea that Sam and I were married and that our kids would be Jewish. The big shock for them was that I wanted to marry Sam. The idea of our kids being Jewish was less traumatic. My parents tried very hard to discourage me from marrying Sam. They pointed out all the problems that could arise and voiced their pessimism about our chances for a successful marriage. Eventually, they resigned themselves to the fact that we were going to get married, but they weren't involved in our wedding plans the way parents of the bride usually are. However, I have to say that they've come around and been very supportive of our decision to raise the boys as Jews."

dren were young, we attended a number of different churches, and the children were introduced to many different ideas about religion. Of course, those ideas were all Christian, but I don't think that what we did was very different from what Keith and Sari are doing."

How would Keith's mother feel if one of her grandchildren chose to have a bar or bat mitzvah? "Well, it would depend on what that meant," she says. "If it meant that the child was becoming a member of the Jewish faith, that would be one thing. But if it meant that he or she was just exploring Jewish roots and ideas, that would be another.

"I know that their other grandmother is very concerned that the children learn more about their Jewish side and get involved in Jewish activities," Keith's mother continues. "I think Keith needs to make sure that she does not apply too much pressure on the children. He and Sari have established a delicate balance between Christian and Jewish ideas, and it could so easily be tipped by outside interference."

"My mother has never been happy with what we have chosen to do," says Sari. "In fact, my parents didn't want me to marry Keith at all. They were so upset that they did everything short of having me kidnapped and deprogrammed. They couldn't get over the fact that I was doing this outrageous thing. I couldn't make them understand that I was marrying Keith because I loved him, not because I wanted to make a statement. I'd have married him no matter what he was.

"My folks were nervous about how we'd fit in socially as a couple," Sari continues. "They had this idea that we'd have two sets of friends, Jewish and Christian, and that the two groups would be mutually exclusive. Of course, that's not the case. In fact, we have lots of friends who are Jewish/Christian couples. Intermarriage is no longer rare or a social taboo."

"I was glad your parents came to our wedding," says Keith. "I'd have felt bad for you if they'd stayed away."

"They came," says Sari, "but they were disappointed. They were hoping that we would have a more traditional Jewish ceremony. I think that they hoped we'd practice more Jewish customs in our home, too."

"When Sari told us that she and Keith were going to raise the children half-and-half, my late husband and I were very upset," Sari's mother says. "How can one child be both Jewish and Christian? It doesn't make any sense to me. I tried to tell her that, but she wouldn't listen. 'This is our decision,' she said very firmly. I cannot help worrying about my grandchildren."

"I think that my mother is overreacting," says Sari. "My children have many of the same experiences that I had as a child. They observe Chanukah and Passover, and they know what Shabbat is. They just have some other experiences as well. The really amazing thing is that my mother has not been an observant Jew for years. She no longer goes to synagogue, and she hasn't kept a kosher kitchen since my dad died. She makes the seder, and that's about it. I don't know why she thinks that she has the right to tell me how to raise my children."

"When Hannah was born," Keith recalls, "Sari's mom offered to make the baby-naming party. I guess I shouldn't have been surprised, since I knew how Sari's parents felt about our not having had Jewish symbols at our wedding. But I thought to myself, 'How can she maintain that these things are important to her if she doesn't do them herself?' "

"I don't claim that I was a perfect mother," says Sari's mom, "but I did the best I knew how. I never had a Jewish education myself. In my time, girls didn't. But I've lived a Jewish life, I know how to run a Jewish home, I make the proper blessings, and I celebrate the holidays. My husband and I brought up our children in the traditional way. Sari is named for my grandmother Sarah. We sent our children to Hebrew school, and they all had a bar or bat mitzvah. Those are the important things. I don't see how Sari can turn her back on our heritage this way."

"My mother cannot understand that Jewish traditions are still important to me," Sari says. "She thinks that our celebrating the Christian holidays lessens the value of the Jewish things we do. She thinks it's hypocritical or crazy to have an Easter brunch in the morning and go to a seder at night. And she doesn't understand that just because a seder is not conducted in the traditional language with the familiar melodies, it's still a seder. She thinks that mixing the two religions is confusing. I think it's broadening."

"I have grandchildren who are being raised as Jews and grandchildren who are Christians," Sari's mother says. "At some point, they'll have to decide whether or not they are going to continue practicing those religions. But how are Sari's children going to know what to keep and what to reject? How are they even going to know where to start looking? They're getting such a mixed message!

"When I offer the children a chance to have a bar or bat mitzvah," she continues, "I'm trying to give them an opportunity to connect with their Jewishness. Children need to know who they are and where they come from. Only then will they have a clear idea of where they're going."

Keith is tolerant of his mother-in-law's views. "I don't think she's really interfering," says Keith. "She just wants the kids to know about Judaism, and that's fine. Even her offering the kids a bar or bat mitzvah is no big deal, because the kids haven't taken her up on it."

Sari is more critical. "I wish she'd just stop it. If one of the kids decides to go ahead with a bar mitzvah someday, great. I'll be as happy as anyone. But right now it's not up for negotiation."

Sari's mother has introduced the children to some Jewish traditions. "I always make a seder," she says, "and every child has a chance to ask the Four Questions. I'm working with little Heather right now, teaching her the Hebrew. At Chanukah I make latkes, we light the menorah, and each child gets a little pocket money. And I try to help Hannah and Charles and Heather understand the rituals that their Jewish cousins observe. Anytime there's a *berit* or a bar mitzvah in the family, we talk about it, and I explain what these occasions mean to Jews. I try not to push, but I want the children to understand more than they do now. They know so little about our heritage. It makes me cry inside."

The children are close to both grandmothers. "Our grandmothers both live in our town, so we get to see them a lot," says Charles. "We're not like some kids who only see their grandparents once or twice a year."

"I really like it when my grandmas tell about when they were little," says Heather. "In those days, Grandma Sadie lived on a street where almost everyone was Jewish. Grandma Lucy didn't know anyone Jewish because there weren't any Jewish people in her town."

The children occasionally attend religious services with each of their grandmothers. "Whenever we go to services with one of our grandmas, it's usually because it's a holiday," says Charles. "It seems as if they want to show off their religion. I know that both of them want us to join their religion, but they don't come right out and say so. They try to show us the best, most fun part of their religion and hope we'll get interested in it."

"I talk with my grandmas about religion," says Hannah. "I ask them about their beliefs and how they were raised. Grandma Lucy told me she went to Sunday school and church and that she can still recite some of the Bible verses that she learned when she was a little girl. And she sings old hymns, but only when no one is around. She thinks that her voice isn't so good any more, but I think it's beautiful.

"It seems strange to me that Grandma Sadie didn't go to Hebrew school," Hannah continues, "especially since her brothers did. She says it just wasn't something that girls did back then. But her mother taught her how to make a Jewish home—to cook kosher food and all. She never had a paying job. She stayed home and raised the children and kept house. She made sure that all of her children went to Hebrew school, including the girls."

"Sometimes I feel as if I'm being pulled between my grand-mas," says Charles. "I mean, Grandma Sadie wants me to have a bar mitzvah. But I know Grandma Lucy wouldn't be too happy if I did. Even though she always says how wonderful it is that we celebrate Chanukah and all that, I think that her feelings would be hurt. I know they're both doing what they think is right, but it's kind of uncomfortable for me."

"Charles will be turning thirteen in a few months," observes Grandma Sadie. "I'm planning to send him a special birthday card with a nice check and a note explaining that this is what I would have given him if he had had a bar mitzvah. I hope that it will make him consider having the ceremony later in life."

Comments

None of these grandparents ever considered the possibility that their child would intermarry. Consequently, their initial reactions varied from mild surprise to strong opposition.

Once they were assured that Keith and Sari's children would not be raised as Jews, Keith's parents gave their blessing. The Jewish grandparents in both families, however, were openly opposed to an interfaith marriage. "Couldn't you have found someone Jewish to marry?" they asked. Sari's mother is hurt and angry that her grandchildren are not being raised as Jews. Sam's parents worry about the depth of Kathy's commitment to the boys' Jewish upbringing. Clearly, for these grandparents, only Jewish grandchildren can insure the continued survival of Judaism. It is painful for them to see the future of their faith embodied in grandchildren who do not think of themselves as Jews.

Once an intermarriage is a reality, most Jewish grandparents are eager to share their heritage with their grandchildren. Sam's parents declare their delight in their grandsons' developing awareness of Jewish culture and rituals, while Sari's mother wishes that she had more opportunities to teach her grandchildren about Judaism.

Most grandparents want to share their holidays, rituals, stories, and history with their grandchildren. Both Sam's and Kathy's parents place a high priority on the presence of their grandchildren at family holiday events. Danny and Zeke take part in Christmas and Easter celebrations with Kathy's family, enjoying the fun and family togetherness. However, the boys are clear about the difference between attending extended-family celebrations of Christian holidays and observing the holidays that are part of their own Jewish tradition.

Kathy's parents do not seem disturbed that their grandsons

are being raised as Jews, but they are concerned that Kathy might abandon her religious beliefs as a result of her participation in Jewish family life. Nonetheless, they actively support Sam and Kathy's efforts to provide their boys with a Jewish upbringing. Kathy's parents are unusually accepting of her decision, and it may be true that they are, as they describe themselves, "more tolerant than most people."

After conceding that she would not be comfortable with the idea of her grandchildren growing up as Jews, Keith's mother graciously accepts that they are being raised with "a few Jewish holidays," along with Christian traditions. Intermarriage does not represent a serious threat to most Protestants because they are the religious majority in America. Therefore, it is not surprising that Kathy's and Keith's parents are not troubled by their child's intermarriage.

To Keith and Sari's dismay, Sari's mother has been very reluctant to accept their decision. She feels strongly about introducing Judaism to her grandchildren, and she regularly invites the grandchildren to participate in Jewish rituals and traditions. Sari and Keith are both surprised by the strength of her conviction because they know that she is a nonobservant Jew.

It often comes as a surprise, particularly to the non-Jewish partner in an intermarriage, how much nonobservant Jewish grandparents want to pass their Judaism on to future generations. Non-Jews find it difficult to believe that someone who has not attended synagogue in years or has not lit Shabbat candles regularly since the last child left home would have any interest in how to raise the grandchildren. What many non-Jews fail to recognize is that Jewish grandparents want to pass on a heritage that puts great emphasis on their people's history, music, literature, ethics, and ties to Israel. They feel they are part of a cultural chain that extends back to biblical times, and they don't want to betray their people by becoming the final link in that chain.

Sari's mother criticizes her daughter for "turning her back on her heritage" and not giving her children a clear religious identity. Sari's mother is really asking where she herself has failed. She worries about her Jewish/Christian grandchildren, but not because she categorically rejects Christianity or even because she insists that her grandchildren be Jewish. Rather, she is concerned about their identity. She asks, "How are they going to know what to keep and what to reject? How are they even going to know where to start looking?" She continually offers the children opportunities to connect with Jewish culture and identify with their Jewish heritage.

Some grandparents are jealous of the influence that the other set of grandparents might have over the grandchildren. They assert a right to "equal time" with the grandchildren, and they worry that the other set of grandparents may make their religion seem superior in some way to their own. Even Kathy's parents, who are supportive of their grandsons' Jewish upbringing, are not above suspicion in the eyes of Sam's parents.

The Cohen and Grayson grandchildren both speak warmly of the special bond they have with their grandparents, although Charles is sometimes uncomfortable with the pressure he feels to meet religious expectations. In most families, the grandparent-child bond is generally strong enough to withstand the stresses of intermarriage.

◆ ◆ ◆ ──────────────────────────────

Chapter 9

The Later Years:
The End of the Life Cycle

- What are some of the issues that arise for interfaith couples at the end of the life cycle?
- How do interfaith couples plan for their own funerals, burials, and mourning rituals?
- How do interfaith couples expect their children to memorialize them?

Introduction

Just as interfaith couples cannot make wedding plans without taking their differences into account, so, too, when these couples begin planning for the end of their lives, they must discuss their attitudes and the family pressures they might encounter.

The best way for an interfaith couple to prepare for the last stage of the life cycle is to begin talking about it early and continue the discussion. They should be as open as possible about their respective expectations and needs concerning their funeral and burial and about their feelings about honoring their partner's requests. In some communities, finding a place where an interfaith couple can be buried together may be a problem. The more decisions a couple makes in advance, the less stress will be experienced by the surviving spouse, who has to handle the burial arrangements.

In addition, it might be wise for couples to think seriously about modern medical technology and how it might affect them. Spouses should know each other's views on organ donation and transplant. They should discuss how they feel about sustaining life by artificial means and how they define that term. Interfaith couples may find that their religious backgrounds have given them different viewpoints on these issues.

Sam and Kathy Cohen

"No one likes to think about dying or having your spouse die," says Sam. "In our case, Kathy could outlive me by fifteen or twenty years. That's as long as we've been married until now."

"If Sam were to die," says Kathy, "I think that the loneliness and sadness would be overwhelming for a while. But I would probably also try to look at that time as an opportunity to do some of the things I don't do now. I'd like to live near the beach, for instance, which Sam hates."

"Sometimes I wonder," says Sam, "whether Kathy would go back to her church and to celebrating the Christian holidays if I died. Of course, I wouldn't be around to say anything about it if she did, but it would be kind of a shame, after all we've done to raise the boys as Jews."

Kathy thinks for a moment. "That's kind of a puzzle. I just don't know what I'd do if Sam died when the boys were still young. It would be pretty hard for me to raise them as Jews by myself. But if the boys were grown up and married, I might still belong to the temple, or I might rejoin my church. Or I might do both—or neither. I just don't know."

"Don't forget," Sam adds, "with any luck, Danny and Zeke and their families will live in the area. I'm sure they'd be observing Jewish traditions to some extent, and I assume you'd spend time with them, especially on holidays. In a way, the roles might be reversed. Maybe in twenty-five years, they'll be the Jewish standard-bearers."

"It's kind of strange," Kathy says, "but after all these years I've gotten used to the rhythm of Jewish life—Shabbat and the cycle of holidays, *berits* and bar mitzvahs. It feels familiar and comfortable now. If I were to keep on observing the Jewish traditions, it wouldn't just be for the kids."

Sam and Kathy have talked about death and dying. "We have living wills and organ donor cards," says Sam. "If we are in a vegetative state, neither of us wants to be kept alive artificially, and we have put that in writing. We have also signed something called a durable power of attorney for health care, which is more binding than a living will in some states and is very explicit about our wishes."

"We've talked with Danny a little bit about the idea of not keeping people alive when they're no longer enjoying life," says Kathy. "As the boys get older, we'll make sure they know what we want to happen to us, where our wills and other papers are, all those things."

The Cohens have also discussed funerals. "I want a traditional Jewish funeral," says Sam, "with a simple closed casket and a graveside service in a Jewish cemetery. That's all. I don't see the point in sitting *shivah* (the mourning period following a funeral). I'd like the boys to light *yahrzeit* candles each year on the anniversary of my death, as a sign of respect and as a remembrance."

"If it is up to me, Sam will have the kind of funeral he wants," Kathy says, "even though sitting *shivah* makes a lot of sense to me. Having family and friends come to remember and pray for the person who died is a welcome expression of ongoing support that has no counterpart in Christian tradition."

What about Kathy's funeral? "That's a hard one," she says. "I've talked to the rabbi about it. He says there's no reason why I couldn't be buried in the Jewish cemetery next to Sam, which is where I'd like to be. He says there's no problem with that, at least at the local Jewish cemetery. I would leave the details of the graveside service up to Sam or the boys. It could be Jewish or nondenominational, whatever they decide. But I also want to have a simple memorial service in my church. Nothing elaborate—just the standard prayers and Bible readings and blessings. I think such a service would be important to my siblings and parents, if they're still alive."

"I understand what you want, and I'll do my best to see that it's done," Sam says, "but you'd better write down specific instructions. I have no idea how to plan a Christian funeral, or even whom to call. My natural reaction would be to plan a Jewish funeral for you, since I see you functioning in a Jewish context most of the time. If you expect a Christian service, that's fine with me, but make sure that you put everything in writing and that you are specific."

Keith and Sari Grayson

"I don't know what religious traditions our kids will choose to observe when they're adults," says Keith. "I do know that we'll stay out of their way. Whatever they decide to do will be fine. As for us, I guess we'll just do whatever seems right at the time."

"It's too hard to predict what will happen," says Sari. "I doubt that Keith would continue celebrating the Jewish holidays if I died, and to tell the truth, I don't know whether I'd celebrate Christmas and Easter if I were alone. It would partly depend on whether the kids would be living nearby and which holidays they would be celebrating."

"My guess is that we would go along with whatever the kids would be doing in terms of holidays and so on," says Keith. "That's what my mom does now. Since my dad died, she comes over here for most of the holidays. She no longer has the energy to celebrate the holidays in her own home."

"We finally got around to making our wills and signing living wills last year," says Sari. "It was hard to talk about what will happen after we die, but it was time to do it. At the same time, we talked about funerals, and that was even harder. We at least agreed about the wills. We had totally different ideas about funerals."

Keith wants a Christian funeral and burial. "I find Christian funerals very reassuring and comforting," he says. "It gives me a sense of peace to think that I'll have an old-fashioned service with some of my favorite hymns and the old familiar words. Of course, I wouldn't be aware that it's happening, but that's what I want."

"I feel just as strongly about having a Jewish funeral," says Sari. "I want an unadorned wooden casket, no music, no service in the chapel—just the traditional burial service by the grave."

"In the past ten years, we've both buried our fathers," says Keith. "I helped my mother with my dad's service, and Sari helped plan her father's. Although neither funeral was fancy, they were very different. At my father's funeral, several people gave very moving eulogies. There were masses of flowers in the church, and the organist played all of Dad's favorite hymns. There were about thirty cars in the funeral procession to the cemetery. My dad had a lot of friends. The minister recited the twenty-third psalm, and then we each tossed a flower on top of the casket after it was lowered. I felt as if I was really saying good-bye to him. The whole thing felt right to me."

Having grown up with a different set of traditions, Sari was uncomfortable at her father-in-law's funeral. "Keith knows how I feel," she says, "and he knows that I wouldn't hurt his feelings for the world. But his father's funeral seemed excessive to me, almost disrespectful. The casket was white and gold and covered with a blanket of flowers. And it was open. I didn't go up to see his dad. I wanted to remember him the way I knew him. To me, the music detracted from the feeling and meaning of the service. The whole thing was more than I thought a funeral should be. It was too much of everything."

"Maybe it's not surprising," says Keith, "but I thought that the service for Sari's dad was almost bleak. The casket was plain wood, not even painted. The service was very short, most of it was in Hebrew, and I wasn't the only one there who didn't understand it. The rabbi gave a short talk, but you couldn't call it a eulogy or a tribute. I don't think he even knew my father-in-law. The whole thing took place in the cemetery. When they lowered the casket, dirt was just shoveled on top of it. Then the service was over. Sari says my father's funeral was too much. To me, her father's was too little, but I know that's the kind of service Sari wants for herself. That's okay with me, although I'd like to see a few more flowers."

"I would be very uncomfortable with the kind of service Keith and his mom planned for his dad," says Sari." All those references to Jesus and heaven aren't for me. Maybe it's because I'm just used to the Jewish service, but that's what I want. And if it is up to me, I will try to arrange the kind of funeral Keith wants."

Where will Keith and Sari be buried? "Of course, we want to be buried next to each other," says Keith. "I know that rules out cemeteries that are exclusively Jewish or Christian. I guess we'll have to find a nonsectarian cemetery. They have those, don't they? We just want to be together where the kids can come and visit us once in a while."

"I hope the children will light *yahrzeit* candles and say *Kaddish* for us," says Sari. "I light candles both for my father and Keith's, and I'd like the children to continue that tradition."

Do the Grayson children know the *Kaddish*, the Jewish prayer for the dead? "They've heard it a few times," says Sari. "They could certainly read the transliteration."

"Or they could say some other prayer," Keith says, "or just make up a prayer if they felt like it. They don't need to say a specific prayer. They could come out to the graveyard and read a poem—maybe Ferlinghetti's "I Am Waiting." However they want to remember us is good enough for me."

"They can read you a poem," says Sari, "but I want them to say *Kaddish* for me."

Comments

There are no automatic answers for the interfaith couple. The process of accommodation and adjustment that begins when an interfaith couple decides to marry continues during the child-rearing years and throughout their life together.

Both couples acknowledge that their observances of family holidays and celebrations might change with the death of one of the partners. The Graysons do not venture to guess what their children will ultimately decide in terms of their own religious affiliation or practice. Keith and Sari say they will follow their children's lead, participating in whatever holidays and rituals the children choose.

The Cohens expect their children to remain Jewish and observe Jewish traditions as they grow up. Sam makes an interesting and optimistic observation when he says of his children, "Maybe in twenty-five years they'll be the Jewish standard-bearers" in the family. Kathy's remark that she might continue to observe Jewish holidays and rituals if they meet her own emotional and spiritual needs is an acknowledgment of how deeply immersed she has become in Jewish tradition. However, she does not rule out the possibility of returning to her church.

When the couples talk together about their own funerals, their different viewpoints clearly emerge. Each of them wants a funeral service consistent with his or her own religious tradition, and their spouses are willing to honor this request. Sam and Kathy demonstrate the kind of accommodation that interfaith couples often make to meet each other's needs. While they agree on their being buried side by side in a Jewish cemetery with a traditional graveside service, Sam is also willing to see to it that Kathy has a Christian memorial service in her church.

Sam's advice to Kathy that she write down specific instructions for her memorial service is good counsel for all interfaith couples. The fact that they grew up in families with different religions usually means that interfaith couples are unfamiliar with each other's traditions and customs. As Sam points out, "I have no idea how to plan a Christian funeral, or even whom to call." Leaving written instructions would be the best way for Keith to insure that his favorite hymns will be played. Making certain that several people know where funeral instructions, wills, and other important documents are kept would also be wise.

After conferring with a rabbi, Sam and Kathy feel certain that their wish to be buried side by side in a Jewish cemetery can be fulfilled. Keith and Sari agree that they will look for a nonsectarian burial ground.

Sam and Sari mention that they would like their children to observe traditional memorial rituals for them. Only Sam, whose children are receiving religious instruction, is certain that his sons will observe *yahrzeit* for him. Sari hopes that even without formal instruction, their children will follow her example of lighting candles and will say prayers for their parents.

As Sam says, "No one likes to think about dying or having your spouse die." Making funeral and burial arrangements in advance prevents disagreements and conflicts about which cemetery will be used, what kind of service will be held, and whether cremation or burial is preferred. Having a written plan to follow frees surviving family members to concentrate on the mourning process instead of on administrative details. Providing precise funeral and burial instructions may be the last and best gift that interfaith partners can give each other.

✦ ✦ ✦ ——————————————————————————

Chapter 10

Problems: When Things Don't Go as Planned

- *What special problems do divorce and remarriage pose for interfaith families?*
- *How do interfaith families fare when faced with an unexpected death?*
- *What happens when an interfaith couple's plan for their children's religious identity does not work out, or when one parent has a change of heart about the children's religious upbringing?*
- *How do interfaith couples respond to their children's dissatisfaction with the religious choices that their parents have made?*

Introduction

When an interfaith couple faces a crisis, previously hidden religious differences may emerge, adding to the existing stress. Sometimes these differences are the root of the problem. Some interfaith couples are not able to overcome the problems they encounter, and they decide to abandon the relationship. But others have found effective, constructive means of coping with such problems as divorce, death, or change of heart.

Divorce and Remarriage

Most young couples marry with the intention of staying together, creating a stable family, and growing old with each other.
Yet nearly one half of the marriages in the United States end
in divorce. Many of them are interfaith relationships. Statistics
show that interfaith couples have a slightly higher divorce rate
than same-faith couples.

Interfaith couples who split up often confront a problem
called "spiritual custody"—having to decide which parent will
have the primary responsibility for their children's religious
training and identity. Spiritual-custody disputes tend to center
around which religious school a child will attend, which life-
cycle events and rituals the child will participate in, and which
holidays the child will celebrate. If conflict over religious practice and ideology contributed to the breakup of the marriage,
spiritual custody of the child can become a major point of con-
tention that may have to be decided by a court. Even when
spiritual custody is not central to the divorce proceedings, a
parent may be reluctant to relinquish whatever influence he or
she has over the child's religious training.

Like many divorced interfaith couples, Mark and Diana
agreed to continue the pattern of religious observance they
had established during their marriage. Mark and Diana had
always celebrated both Jewish and Christian holidays with their
children. Since the couple's divorce, their children have spent
Chanukah and Passover with Mark and Christmas and Easter
with Diana. Since neither Mark nor Diana feels strongly about
the children's having a formal religious education, they agreed
not to send the children to either a church school or Hebrew
school. The children continue to identify themselves as "half-
Jewish, half-Christian," just as they did when their parents lived
together.

Paul and Lisa have had a harder time resolving the issue of
the spiritual custody of their seven-year-old son, Josh. While
they were married, Paul agreed to raise Josh as a Jew and
participated to a small extent in the family's Jewish observances. When Josh was four, Lisa enrolled him in religious

school at her synagogue and began taking him to occasional services.

Now that Paul and Lisa have separated, Paul no longer wants Josh to be raised as a Jew. "He's my son," Paul says, "and that makes him half-Christian." Against Lisa's wishes, Paul has begun taking Josh to church services on the two weekends a month that they spend together.

Lisa is angry and bitter. "Paul agreed that Joshua would be raised as a Jew," she says. "It's too late for him to change his mind. Things are messed up enough with the divorce. This is just going to confuse Josh more."

Neither parent is willing to relinquish spiritual custody of their son, and the family may be headed for court. Josh will not talk about the situation.

Bart and Mimi were married for ten years. They split up when Susan was ten and Eli was seven. "We had always observed both sets of holidays," Mimi says. "It just seemed like the right thing to do. But after Bart left, I felt that I didn't want to celebrate Christmas and Easter anymore. I had done it because it was important to Bart, but it's completely contrary to how I was raised and who I am. We're functioning more like a Jewish family now that Bart is gone. The only thing the kids do that's not Jewish is spend Christmas with their father."

Mimi and the children have joined a synagogue, whose religious school the children attend. Both children identify themselves as Jews and seem to enjoy the family's Jewish rituals. Their father comments, "The kids are living with Mimi, so I guess she's entitled to make those decisions. As long as I get them on Christmas, it's okay with me."

Mary and Nat divorced when their boys were eight and five. For the past three years, Mary has had the children during the school year, and they have spend every summer with Nat. "Nat said he wanted to expose the boys to Judaism," Mary explains, "and that's okay with me. But he lives in an area where there's no synagogue, no Jewish community, nothing. Nat complains because they go to church with me. He says that the kids aren't getting an equal dose of Judaism. But the kids refer to themselves as Presbyterians. I know that I'm not going to stop taking them to church. If the issue is important enough to their father, he'll figure something out."

A parent's remarriage can be as traumatic for a child as her parents' divorce was. Children commonly fantasize that their parents will get back together. Some even scheme and plot toward that end. Remarriage destroys the child's dream that her parents will reunite.

The term "blended family" describes the myriad combinations of parents and stepparents, children and stepchildren, siblings, stepsiblings, and half siblings that are created by remarriage. The results of both intermarriage and remarriage can be remarkably complicated and challenging.

Linda and Steve are a fairly typical blended family. Linda and her first husband, who are both Jewish, divorced when their sons were four and six. Two years later, Linda married Steve, a Christian. The boys live with Linda and Steve and visit their father during vacations. Although Steve does not want to convert to Judaism, he is willing to participate in Jewish holidays and rituals with Linda and the boys. "It's their religion, and it's okay with me," he says. "But if Linda and I ever have our own child, I'd want to do something different. I don't think it would be right for my own child to be raised Jewish." Both Linda and Steve recognize the need to resolve this issue before they have a child together.

For Sid and Tracy, the issue was not how to raise the child they had together but how to raise Sid's son from his first marriage. Sid and Tracy are both Jewish, and both had been previously married to Christians. Shortly after they married, Sid's nine-year-old son John left his Christian mother's home and came to live with them. Within a year, Sid and Tracy had a baby girl. "I felt like an ogre telling John that we weren't going to celebrate Christmas," says Tracy, "but we're a Jewish family, and we don't do that. I'm sorry, but John just has to get used to the fact that he's living in a Jewish family and that he has to abide by our customs. I think Sid would make a Christmas celebration for him, but I'm really uncomfortable with the idea. Besides, we're trying to teach our daughter that we're Jewish and that it's great to be Jewish. Celebrating Christmas would just confuse her."

Pat and Jeanne's case of "yours, mine, and ours" has an interfaith twist. Pat, who is Jewish, had two daughters with his first wife, a Christian. The children were preschoolers when their parents divorced. Jeanne, who was raised in the Catholic church, had been married to an evangelical Protestant and had converted to his religion before their son was born. Jeanne and her first husband were divorced when their son was in elementary school. At about that time, Jeanne became interested in Judaism and began thinking about converting.

When Pat and Jeanne met, each had part-time custody of their children, all of whom were being raised as Christians. Shortly after they married, Jeanne converted to Judaism. All of the children visited them regularly and celebrated Jewish holidays with them. Within a few years, Pat and Jeanne had two daughters of their own, along with full-time custody of Pat's two girls and partial custody of Jeanne's son. Because Pat's children had spent many years observing Christian holidays with their mother and because Jeanne's son was usually with them during his winter vacation, Pat and Jeanne reluctantly added a modest Christmas celebration to their observance of Jewish holidays.

The family joined a synagogue, and all four girls were enrolled in religious school. Gradually, Pat's daughters began to consider themselves Jews. Meanwhile, the family continued to celebrate Christmas, although the only Christian among them was Jeanne's son. It wasn't until the oldest girl was studying for her bat mitzvah that the family stopped observing Christmas. Now when Jeanne's son is with them at Christmastime, he has a small tree in his own room. Looking back, Jeanne acknowledges that she had not been ready to give up celebrating Christmas until several years after she had chosen to become a Jew.

The possible combinations of marriage, divorce, intermarriage, and remarriage are endless and can create unique situations for children. Will is a case in point. His mother, Suzanne, is an Episcopalian and his father, Chuck, is Jewish. They divorced when Will was a toddler. Both parents soon remarried, each to a Christian who did not attend church. From the time he was two years old until his high school graduation, Will divided his time between the two households, spending the first half of every week with his Christian mother and stepfather and the latter part of each week in his father's interfaith home.

Neither of Will's parents tried to wield exclusive influence over their son's religious identity. They have made it clear to him that his religion would be his choice. "It was sticky enough working out the joint-custody issue," says Suzanne. "I thought that trying to address the religious issue would put the kibosh on the whole arrangement."

Will has celebrated Christian holidays in both households and has attended some Christian services, but he has not had any formal religious education. "I've taken Will to church with me on Christmas and Easter now and then," Suzanne says. "He's gone to a few bar mitzvahs, but he hasn't ever been to regular synagogue services. I don't think he sees himself as belonging to any particular religion."

As a teenager, Will started visiting the homes of some of his Jewish friends on Friday evenings. "It took me a long time to figure out that he was going there to participate in the Jewish Sabbath," says Suzanne. "Maybe he's beginning to explore the options that are open to him. Even though we weren't able to give him a clear religious identity, he's a very ethical person. I hope he'll find a religion that is consistent with his values."

When a Parent Dies

An unexpected death is traumatic for every family. The religious differences within an interfaith family can intensify the crisis, both immediately after the death and in the months and years that follow.

Virtually every religion includes burial and mourning customs that were meant to help survivors cope with the loss of a loved one. Following familiar rituals can provide a family with comfort and support after a sudden death. In an interfaith family, however, conflict over burial and mourning rituals can add to the stress of an already traumatic time.

Cleo, who is Protestant, and her Jewish husband, Len, were married for fifteen years and had three children. They agreed to raise their children with some observances from each faith but with no definite religious identification. When the children were seven, nine, and thirteen, Len was killed in an accident.

Although Len and Cleo had never discussed funeral arrangements, Cleo was sure that Len would have wanted a Jewish burial service. "I was in a state of shock," she says. "I didn't know where to turn. I called a Jewish mortuary, and they pretty much took over. I didn't know a rabbi, so the mortuary called one for us. The rabbi wanted to find out a little about Len so that he could say a few words at the service. There I was, only twelve hours after Len was killed, trying to describe him to a total stranger. Then suddenly, I realized that if Len was going to be buried in a Jewish cemetery, I'd have to be buried there, too, if I wanted to be next to him. I needed time to think that over, but there was no time. The mortuary people were telling us that Jewish law requires that he be buried within twenty-four hours. That didn't give me much time to think things through. It was a nightmare."

After Len's death, Cleo found it difficult to observe any of the Jewish traditions in her home. "We had always lit the Chanukah candles and done a few other Jewish things," she says. "But without Len, I didn't feel like doing them. I had to tell the kids that it was too hard for me to do those things without their father. It took a while, but I think they understood."

Cleo's oldest daughter says, "When Dad was alive, we had Chanukah and sometimes Passover, and once in a while we'd go to the synagogue. Now we go to our cousins' bar mitzvahs and things like that, but we only have Christian holidays at home. I think that doing Jewish things reminds Mom too much of Dad. Besides, she doesn't really know all that much about Jewish holidays."

"I know that sharing his heritage with the kids was important to Len," says Cleo. "But I am not able to do that. I feel bad because the kids are half-Jewish, and they're not getting any Jewish training. The only way I know to introduce them to Jewish culture and ideas would be for me to join a synagogue, and I would find that very uncomfortable.

"When Len was alive, our approach to religion was very casual," Cleo continues. "We just did whatever we felt like at the time. Now I wish we had been a little more structured. We had never developed any family traditions. I think that if we had, losing Len wouldn't have been so hard."

Judith and Karl had decided to raise their daughter Becky as a Jew, although Karl is not Jewish. Judith died when Becky was five. "It was very sudden and unexpected," Karl says. "The people at Judith's synagogue were extremely helpful in making funeral arrangements, and so on. I didn't know the first thing about Jewish funerals, and they took care of a lot of things I was too numb to do."

Now Karl is struggling to fulfill his commitment to raise his nine-year-old daughter as a Jew. "When Judith said that she wanted to raise our kids in her religion, I agreed," says Karl, "but I always assumed that Judith would be here to carry the main load, to do the holidays and everything else. When Judith died, I wondered how on earth I could continue observing the Jewish traditions without her. I thought about just letting the matter drop, but I didn't want to pull the rug out from under Becky. It was really rough on her, losing her mom at such a young age. I didn't want her to lose her religion, too. So I still take her to religious school at the synagogue, and we still celebrate Jewish holidays at home.

"It's tough sometimes," he continues. "I've had to learn much more than I ever expected to about Jewish holidays and customs. I've actually learned a lot from Becky. She brings information home from religious school and teaches me. I don't know if she'll remain involved in Judaism as an adult, but at least I've done my part."

Tom and Rene had been married for only four years when Tom died. "The only kind of burial service I knew about was Jewish," Rene says. "I'd never been to a Christian funeral. When Tom died, his mother and I went to what was supposed to be a nonsectarian funeral home, and I read the service they normally used. I was shocked! It was full of references to Jesus and heaven—things that I couldn't accept at all, things that I knew Tom hadn't even believed in. So along with trying to cope with the fact that I had lost my husband, I had to fight with the funeral people and Tom's family for the kind of service I wanted. We finally agreed to omit all the references to Jesus and to use psalms and parts of the Torah, or what they call the Old Testament. His parents are still upset that I wouldn't agree to any passages from the New Testament."

Tom and Rene did not have children. "We were just starting to talk about having kids when Tom got sick," Rene says. "I said that I wanted the kids to at least know about their Jewish heritage, and Tom said that he didn't want them to miss out on Santa Claus and all that. I guess we would have decided on doing a half-and-half thing. But I don't know what I would have done if we had already had kids when he died. I don't think I'd be comfortable celebrating the Christian holidays without a Christian partner."

When a Child Dies

It has been said that when a parent dies, the past is lost, but when a child dies, the future is lost. The death of a child is one of the most stressful events that any couple can experience. The strain is possibly greater for an intermarried couple than for a same-faith couple.

Diane and Larry are raising their children as Christians, although Larry is a Jew. "Larry is supportive of my taking the kids to church, and we celebrate Christian traditions and holidays as a family," Diane says.

A few years ago, Larry and Diane lost a young son. "Anyone who has ever been through such an experience will tell you how devastating it is," Diane says. "Everything seems unreal, and you keep wishing you could wake up from this bad dream. At the hospital, they asked us what kind of funeral we were going to have. I wanted a Christian funeral for Jon. It didn't seem to matter much to Larry.

"I felt as if the funeral was my only chance to say good-bye to our son. It was very meaningful to me," Diane continues. "I think the fact that we had already talked about what kind of funeral we wanted for ourselves made it a little easier to talk about a service for Jon. Larry knew how important having a Christian funeral is to me, so it didn't come as a total shock to him that I wanted one for our son. In a way, that made a hard time a little easier for me."

Maria and Mike had two girls and were hoping for a boy. "Maybe it's an old-fashioned idea," says Mike, "but I wanted to have a son and give him a *berit* and a bar mitzvah, like I had. Even though Maria's Catholic, she agreed to go along with both ceremonies if we had a boy."

Maria became pregnant when their daughters were three and five. "It was a normal pregnancy in every way," says Maria. "The birth was easy, and we thought that everything was fine. We named our son Adam. But it turned out that he had a heart defect, and there was nothing anyone could do to save him. He lived for five and a half months."

"The day that he died was the worst day of my life," says Mike. "We were both devastated. I knew that I should have been more supportive of Maria, but I was so torn up I had nothing left to give. We wanted him so much, and he was gone so quickly. When he died, it was very important to me that he be buried according to Jewish custom."

"When Mike said that he wanted to give Adam a Jewish service, I was too numb to care," says Maria. "I think I said, 'Do whatever you want.' "

"All the time that I was making the burial arrangements," says Mike, "the tears streamed down my face. I couldn't believe I was burying my son. And my in-laws made it worse by trying to get us to have a Catholic funeral. I just refused to discuss it."

"I went through those days in a stupor," says Maria. "I don't remember eating anything or sleeping or talking to anyone. I don't remember any of the service, but I remember how quiet it was at the cemetery. And I remember feeling completely empty and drained when we left."

"We went through a really tough period after we lost Adam,"

says Mike. "His death exposed some areas of our relationship that needed work but that we'd been ignoring. We went through several months of counseling, dealing both with the baby's death and our own problems."

"I would never wish such an experience on anyone," says Maria, "but for us, it was a watershed. We couldn't ignore the fact that things weren't going well. We had to deal with them. We got some help, and we made it."

Two years after Adam's death, Mike and Maria had a healthy baby boy. They still belong to a support group for parents who have lost a child. "We look around the group and feel really lucky," says Maria. "Lots of couples can't handle a child's death, and they eventually break up."

"You never expect your child to die before you do," Mike points out. "It turns your world upside down. The death of a child can magnify the weaknesses in a relationship, but it can also bring out the strengths."

Alan and Marlene faced a similar crisis, but their relationship was not able to survive it. "I'm what you might call a cultural Jew," says Alan, "and my ex-wife Marlene was raised as a Methodist, although she'd probably describe herself as an agnostic. When the kids were little, we tried to practice a little of each religion. You know, we had a Christmas tree and a menorah, that kind of thing. The kids seemed to like what we did."

When the couple's children were ten and eight, Marlene became pregnant. "Marlene and I had waited a long time to have another baby," says Alan. "The kids were growing up, and we really wanted one more, but it took a long time. When she finally got pregnant, we were ecstatic. I asked Marlene if we could name the baby in the synagogue, even though we hadn't done that with the other kids, and she agreed. We took the baby to my parents' synagogue, and we named her Rosalind, after my grandmother Rachel. I don't think Marlene had ever been in a synagogue before, but she was receptive and seemed to enjoy the ceremony."

When Rosalind was four months old, she died of Sudden Infant Death Syndrome. "She just didn't wake up one morning," says Alan. "You hear about SIDS, but you never think that it will happen to your baby. I can't begin to tell you how much guilt and anger I felt. I kept asking myself what I had done, what Marlene had done, how we could have prevented this death. Of course, intellectually I knew that it wasn't anyone's fault. But we never could talk about it. We couldn't get past the anger and guilt and blame."

Their daughter's death created a crisis in Alan and Marlene's marriage. "It brought out resentments that both Marlene and I had been harboring for years. We went to a counselor, but that just seemed to bring out even more differences. For instance, during counseling, Marlene told me she was furious that I had arranged a Jewish burial for Rosie. At the time, she had gone along with the idea, but later she was mad. She said that it was 'too Jewish.' "

He shakes his head. "I don't know. Maybe it took some time for the reality of Rosie's death to sink in before Marlene knew how she felt. But something had to be done at the time, and I did it the only way I knew how. I'd probably do it again, too, because giving my child a Jewish burial seemed to me to be the right thing to do. But it was a problem for Marlene. It was one of the things that caused our breakup."

Since their divorce, Alan and Marlene have shared custody of their children. At Marlene's house, the children celebrate Christmas and Easter. When they are with Alan, they participate in Jewish holidays and rituals. "I'd like to send them to Hebrew school," says Alan, "but I don't know how Marlene would react. It's a very sore point."

When an Agreement Doesn't Work

Sometimes, despite an interfaith couple's conscientious attempts to reach and maintain a religious consensus within their family, they find that they cannot keep the pact they have made. Whether an agreement is broken because it is too difficult to keep or because one parent has a religious change of heart, the result can be traumatic.

"Even before we were married, Cecelia and I had said we

would bring our children up in both religions," says Jed. "And our first child was both baptized and named in the temple. Our plan was to continue doing the rituals of both religions, send the children to both Christian and Jewish religious schools, take them to church and temple—the whole thing. It just didn't work out."

"My parents were thrilled that we had Sarah baptized," says Cecelia. "If you come from a Catholic family as I do, you know how important baptism is. I think that Jed's family was unhappy about the baptism, but we had the naming ceremony in the temple, and that placated them a little."

"When Sarah was little, we started taking her to church and to temple," says Jed. "I had always enjoyed going to Cecelia's church. The people are very friendly, and I did not feel that they expected me to convert. Cecelia was accepted at the temple in which I grew up. We thought that everything was fine. When Sarah was five, she started to attend temple school on Saturday mornings and church school on Sundays."

"At both the church and temple she learned about Noah's ark, Adam and Eve, and Daniel in the lion's den," says Cecelia. "She learned the Ten Commandments and various Bible stories that both Jed and I knew. That was okay with both of us. We could all talk about those things together."

"But then," says Jed, "she started bringing home certain ideas from Sunday school that bothered me. As long as we were on common ground, like talking about Noah and Moses and the Golden Rule, it was fine, but when she began to talk about how the stories in the Old Testament proved that Jesus was the messiah, I couldn't handle it."

"The fact is, Sarah couldn't handle it, either," says Cecelia. "We hadn't thought about what would happen when she started getting double messages, like Jesus both was and wasn't the messiah. She was getting very confused and upset. We realized that she was too little to be able to decide which stories were analogies and which were real and that we weren't helping her by telling her that she was both religions. As a result, we felt we had to decide whether we wanted to bring her up Christian or Jewish."

"Despite the lobbying of Cecelia's parents, we chose Judaism," says Jed. "I think that our decision was based mainly on the fact that Cece's more comfortable with Jewish ideas and customs than I am with Christianity. Our son had a *berit* but was not baptized, which still irks Cece's parents."

"They're more than irked," says Cecelia. "They feel they've been tricked. It was okay with them when we were raising the kids both Christian and Jewish. I guess they figured that the kids would be more Christian because our society is Christian. I've tried to explain to them that our plan just didn't work out. It seemed very reasonable and logical when we decided on it, but it just wasn't realistic."

"Of course, my mother is very pleased with the way things worked out," says Jed. She doesn't understand that it was not a contest. We had tried something and it didn't work out, so we moved to Plan B. I wish both our families would understand that there are no winners or losers in all of this."

"I don't know if I'll ever be able to patch things up between my parents and me," Cecelia says sadly. "The only thing that they think could have been worse would have been if I had converted to Judaism. They're probably expecting that to happen any day. They undoubtedly think that's the next step, even though it probably won't happen."

Jed and Cecelia recognized that their original plan was not working, and they agreed to try another. But not all couples are able to agree on whether a plan of theirs is succeeding. For instance, Bill and Paula had agreed to raise their two daughters as Unitarians. "I wasn't in touch with being Jewish at all then," says Bill. "Paula, who was raised in a Protestant denomination, wanted to take the girls to a Unitarian church, and that was fine with me. In fact, I went, too."

"We all went to the Unitarian church," says Paula. "It conveyed a very strong moral and ethical message, without emphasizing any particular religion. Unitarianism seemed to provide us with the perfect way to give our children a strong set of values without our having to deal with the differences between our religious backgrounds."

Then Bill rediscovered his Jewish roots. "When our older daughter was three, I started to feel a need to get back to Judaism and to introduce her to it. It bothered me that she wasn't being taught any Jewish values or culture. I told Paula that I wanted to start celebrating Jewish holidays and taking the girls to temple sometimes. It has caused somewhat of a problem."

Paula is bothered by Bill's sudden interest in Judaism. "We made an agreement," she points out. "I don't expose the girls to the religion I grew up with. I don't talk about Jesus, even at Christmas and Easter. So I feel that Bill should avoid teaching the girls about his religion. He should have asked himself how important Judaism was to him before the girls were born instead of waiting until now to 'rediscover his roots,'" she says, making quotation marks with her fingers. "If he's going to introduce the girls to Judaism, I should have the chance to introduce them to Christianity. That seems only reasonable."

"We made our agreement in good faith," Bill says. "But things change. Judaism's important to me now, at least culturally. I'm not that interested in the kids' having a religion per se, but I do want them to know about their Jewish heritage. I don't necessarily want to teach them the religious parts of Judaism, just the values and history and maybe about some of the ceremonies, holidays, and customs. That's not necessarily religious."

"It's Judaism," Paula maintains, "and if you're going to teach them about Jewish traditions, then they need to learn about Christian traditions, too. I hate to sound like a politician demanding equal time, but that's what seems equitable to me."

Eva and Tony face a similar situation. "Tony was completely disinterested in religion when we got married," says Eva, "even though his parents are church members and he was brought up in a Protestant home. He agreed to our getting married in the synagogue, to naming the children there, and to raising our children as Jews. Although he wasn't involved in the synagogue, he was never opposed to my going and taking the kids. But when the kids were in elementary school, he became a born-again Christian, and our lives were turned inside out. Suddenly, he started objecting to the kids' going to temple and Hebrew school. He wants them to go to church with him, and he's very concerned about the fact that they haven't accepted Jesus as their savior.

"I know Tony's doing what he thinks is right," she continues, "but it's very confusing for the children. Our son is now thirteen and pretty secure in his Judaism, but he gets upset when his father starts telling him that Jesus died for our sins and that every person needs the forgiveness of Christ. It goes against his Jewish training. Our nine-year-old daughter is feeling very mixed up. She doesn't want to hurt me by going to church with her dad, and she doesn't want to displease him by going to temple. She no longer knows whom or what to believe or who she is. It's a mess."

Eva goes on. "In every other way, our family life is fine. It's just the religious aspect, the part that's supposed to be good and positive and bring you together, that's become a problem. I respect Tony's right to follow his own religion, but I wish he'd leave us out of it."

Both Paula and Eva feel that their partners reneged on an important promise. They feel deceived and hurt. Paula says, "I stuck to my end of the bargain. Why can't he?"

Both women also have a hard time believing in the sincerity of their spouses' sudden interest in religion. "How could religion be so important to him now, after years of not caring about it?" Eva asks. "Now it's the biggest thing in Tony's life. I have a hard time accepting that."

"I suspect this interest in Judaism is a phase that Bill is going through," says Paula. "I doubt that it will last long. It just bothers me that he's so adamant about bringing the girls into it, after we agreed not to impose either of our religions on them."

Neither Bill nor Tony set out deliberately to undermine the agreement they had made about the religious identity of their children. But having children brought Bill in touch with parts of his religious/cultural identity that he had ignored for years. And Tony now feels a sincere need to share the ideas and answers he has found in Christianity with his children. Unfortunately, the genuine and positive religious impulses of both fathers are creating serious difficulties for their families.

Chuck and Maryanne's situation is slightly different. "I was raised a Methodist," says Maryanne, "but Christianity never made much sense to me. When I married Chuck and started learning about Judaism, I was very struck by how much more reasonable Judaism is. I had no trouble agreeing to raise our kids as Jews."

"I wasn't surprised when Maryanne said that she was thinking of converting," says Chuck. "But I am surprised at how observant she's become since the conversion. She has enrolled the kids in Hebrew school. On Friday nights we welcome Shabbat at home first and then rush through dinner so that we can get to the synagogue in time for services. We celebrate all the Jewish holidays in the book, including some I'm not even familiar with. Frankly, this is more Judaism than I had bargained for. We can't even go away for the weekend because the kids would miss religious school."

"Chuck wants the kids to be Jewish, and so do I," says Maryanne. "You can't make them Jewish just by deciding that's what they'll be. You have to do things. You have to practice Judaism if you want to give your kids a strong foundation. It's not as though I'm making us into super-Jews. We don't keep kosher, spend most of Saturday at the synagogue, insist that the boys wear hats all the time, or anything like that. To tell the truth, I think that what we're doing is the bare minimum."

"It's still more than I ever thought I'd be doing," Chuck says. "I probably wouldn't be doing all this if I'd married a woman who had been born Jewish."

When the Children Want to Change Their Parents' Arrangement

The best-laid plans of parents are sometimes rejected by the very people those plans were meant to serve. Some children choose to follow a path different from the one their parents selected.

Stan and Martha met at work and were immediately attracted to each other, but Martha declined several invitations to go out with Stan. "I was very uncomfortable with the idea of dating someone outside my faith," Martha explains. "I knew that he was Jewish, and I'd never dated a Jew, although I'd known some. But he kept asking me, and I finally said yes. It didn't take long before we were engaged."

They were married in Martha's church but only after they had agreed that their children would not be exposed to any formal religion. Martha and Stan decided to let their children choose their own faith when they were old enough.

When their oldest child, Mark, was seven, he asked why all his friends went to Sunday school and he didn't. Martha and Stan explained their decision and told him that when he and his brothers were old enough, they could choose a religion. "At that point," says Stan, "we thought the matter was closed. Little did we know that Mark was going around the neighborhood pumping his friends for information about what Sunday school was like and wangling invitations to go to church with other families."

"We realized that we had to do something," says Martha. "Otherwise, we would have no say in what religion he might choose. He might decide that being a Moonie or something like that suited him best, and we didn't want that."

Martha and Stan took all the children to visit several churches and the synagogue in their neighborhood. "It was obvious where we belonged," says Martha. "When we went to one particular church, we encountered half of our friends from the neighborhood, from Scouts, and from the kids' sports teams. Everyone was there."

"I was definitely not keen on joining a church," says Stan. "But it seemed to be a family-type place, so we joined as a family. Although the whole thing did not work out the way we had planned, the kids have a great time at the church, and Martha is very comfortable there, so it's fine with me. But I am not a Christian and never will be one."

"We always said that we'd let the kids decide when they were old enough," says Martha. "It just so happened that for Mark, seven was old enough."

Chris and Michelle had a similar experience. Chris, who is Jewish, and Michelle, who was brought up Protestant, agreed to raise their children with the "best of both religions." "We told the kids that they were half-Jewish, half-Christian," says Chris, "and we celebrated all the holidays—Christmas and Chanukah and Passover and Easter."

"It didn't seem like a big deal at the time," says Michelle. "It just seemed like the logical thing to do."

"When Owen, our oldest, was seven, he started asking questions like 'Who is God?' " says Chris. "He'd ask things like 'If we're half-Christian, why don't we go to church half the time?' We were floored."

"We really didn't have any answers," says Michelle. "We realized that we had to reexamine our plan. I mean, if Owen, at seven, could see the inconsistencies in what we were doing, we thought we'd better take another look at the plan."

Chris and Michelle visited churches and synagogues, looking for a place in which they both felt comfortable. "We ended up joining a nearby synagogue," says Chris. "It's very different from what I grew up with, but Michelle and the kids felt accepted there. We joined almost immediately."

"This will be our first December without Christmas," says Michelle. "The kids are more relaxed about that prospect than I am. They're really excited about celebrating the Jewish holidays and observing the traditions they're studying in religious school. They're not even talking about Christmas—only about Chanukah and the meaning of all the rituals, which they didn't know before."

Michelle pauses before continuing. "To tell the truth, I'm thinking about converting. The more I learn about Judaism, the more it makes sense to me. It is concerned with all the things that are important to me: justice, taking care of less fortunate people, even ecology. I also find observing Jewish rituals and customs very satisfying. Probably by this time next year, we'll be a completely Jewish family. And all because our child asked a few questions!"

Chris and Michelle, like Stan and Martha, changed their family's religious orientation in response to one of their children's questions and interest. Other families have chosen to stick to their original plan, despite their children's criticisms. Hannah, Sari and Keith's sixteen-year-old daughter, does not appreciate her parents' decision to include a few practices from each religion. "You'd think they could have come up with a better solution than that," she grumbles. "It seems to me that they didn't want to go to the trouble of choosing a religion because that would have been difficult and someone's feelings might have been hurt. So instead, they decided to celebrate a couple of holidays from each religion."

Hannah's parents accept her indignation calmly. "We did our best," says Keith. "In the long run, all of our kids will do what they want to anyway. We decided on what we thought was the best approach. If Hannah's upset about our decision, I assume she'll do whatever's necessary to make her own."

Sari concurs. "I think Hannah will eventually see she was very lucky that she was raised with two religions. She knows about both traditions, two sets of holidays, and two ways of looking at things. She's just going through a rebellious stage. She'll get over it."

Keith and Sari do not plan to change their family's religious observances because of Hannah's dissatisfaction. "In the first place, we've been doing things this way for over fifteen years," says Sari. "We have family traditions that we love, and we're not going to change them. In the second place, the other children are perfectly content with the way we do things. They don't seem to think we've made a big mistake. And finally, Keith and I are happy with our life. We got married because we like each other the way we are. We agreed to share our religions and not to try and change each other. That's what we've done."

"I'm sure it's not easy for people in mixed marriages to talk about this issue," Hannah acknowledges, "but it sure seems as if my parents just avoided it instead of trying to work it out. And what do we kids have? Nothing. We know a little bit about both Christianity and Judaism but not enough to feel that we are a part of either."

Comments

All couples, whether of the same faith or of different faiths, encounter changes and challenges during their years together. Divorce, death, change of mind and heart are all issues that may escalate to crisis proportions when partners hold different religious outlooks and observe different traditions.

There are no easy solutions for an interfaith family facing a crisis. Even a couple for whom religion poses no problem when things are going well may be overwhelmed by conflicts resulting from religious differences during times of severe stress.

It has been said that crisis equals opportunity. Whether a problem becomes a catastrophe depends on a couple's ability to keep communication lines open, adjust their expectations to new realities, and be sensitive to each other's religious background and beliefs.

Chapter 11

Two Families: A Last Look

- *How do the two interfaith couples evaluate their decision about how to raise their children?*
- *Do they have any regrets about their choice?*
- *How have the children of these interfaith couples been affected by their parents' decision?*

Introduction

Raising children requires an investment of time, thought, money, and energy. Most parents measure the rate of return on their investment in terms of how well their expectations for the kind of life their family will lead have been met. Both the Cohens and Graysons have had several years to implement their decision about how they will raise their children. How do they think things are going?

Sam and Kathy Cohen

"As time goes by," says Kathy, "I'm more and more pleased that we decided to do it this way. Judaism gives us a lot as a family: holidays, rituals, a community. And the kids are developing a strong moral sense. Most important, they like being Jewish."

"Judaism is a big part of the boys' lives," says Sam, "and I'm enjoying being part of the Jewish community again. At first, I thought I wanted the boys to be nonreligious, cultural Jews. But now I think that the only way a person can become a cultural Jew is by having a traditional upbringing, which includes going to temple and practicing the rituals. How can a person who has no Jewish background truly understand the significance of Jewish art or music or even food? I mean, what's the point of eating matzah if you don't know anything about its history and symbolism?"

"Our kids feel that they are part of Jewish history and culture," says Kathy. "I like the fact that they're getting a good foundation in Jewish values, which stress working for justice. I'm also glad we're exposing the kids to the spiritual side of Judaism. I was really touched when we went to parents' day at Danny's Jewish camp last summer and the first thing he wanted to show us was the open-air chapel. It overlooked the ocean, and the back of the ark opened to the sea and sky. I thought the place had a very spiritual feeling, and it seemed to me that Danny felt that way, too.

"I've come to regard being Jewish as something special, even precious, yet I haven't converted. It's not that I've never considered it. I do at times, like when I'm preparing a seder or when we're talking about the boys' bar mitzvahs. But I don't feel right about rejecting my past."

"We've talked about Kathy's converting," says Sam, "and it wouldn't surprise me if she someday decided to become a Jew. I think the message it would send to the boys—that our religion is so special that she chose to join us—would be a strong and wonderful one."

"I'm sure the boys will ask me at some point why I've never converted if Judaism is so wonderful that I wanted them to be Jewish," Kathy says. "When they ask, I'll probably tell them that it was very important to me that they have a religious foundation and that they have strong roots in a tradition. And I'll tell them that part of the reason it's so important to me is because I value my own roots and the traditions I grew up with. They need to know that their dad and I had to make a choice, and we chose Judaism because we could all participate in it together. Whether I ever convert or not, I feel really good about having helped give the boys this religious tradition and heritage."

"If Kathy ever did convert," says Sam, "it would have to be because she wanted to, because becoming Jewish was meaningful to her. I know her well enough to say that it would be because Judaism had become spiritually satisfying to her."

"I think it's a mistake to convert to please your spouse or to be like your kids or to appease your in-laws," Kathy says. "I've known people who have changed their religion for all of those reasons, and they usually reverted to their old religion. The people I know who have adopted a new faith and stayed with it forever are the ones who were responding to an inner need instead of to external pressure. Right now, I'm very comfortable participating in Jewish observances both at home and in the temple. I am accepted and valued just the way I am.

"I feel as though there's a continuum," Kathy continues. "At one end there is absolutely no connection with Judaism and at the other end is conversion. I've moved a very long way along that continuum, and I'm probably now more than halfway toward the conversion end. Maybe someday, I'll find myself completing the journey. If I do, I know the Jewish community will be ready, willing, and able to accept me as a Jew."

"Things have changed since I was a kid," says Sam. "Back then, I doubt a non-Jewish parent would have been accepted as an active member of a synagogue. Of course, back then the intermarriage rate wasn't fifty percent. The Jewish community has had to change with the times."

The Cohens visited several temples before making their choice. "We visited every temple within twenty miles of our house," says Kathy, "and we discovered that they were very different in their attitude toward interfaith families. We joined the one in which we felt the most comfortable and the one that had the most liberal policy about a non-Jewish family member participating in activities and services."

"We also chose the one that gave us the warmest welcome," says Sam. "We realized that if we wanted our kids to feel comfortable in a temple, we also had to feel comfortable there."

"We ended up choosing a temple with a very high percentage of interfaith families," Kathy says. "Almost forty percent of the families in our congregation have a member who was not born Jewish. Many of these members have converted, but there are quite a few active non-Jewish members who may never convert. Our temple also has very well-attended adult education classes, in which both Jews and non-Jews can learn more about Jewish traditions. These classes are not conversion classes, but many of the non-Jewish spouses who attend them do convert once they learn more about Judaism."

"Our rabbi is very supportive of interfaith families," says Sam. "He also understands people like me who left organized religion after their bar or bat mitzvah and then felt a need to get involved again after they had kids. He never asked where I had been all those years. The funny thing is that I enjoy the people and the activities and even the services much more than I thought I would."

Do Sam and Kathy have any regrets about their decision?

"No," says Sam. "Things haven't turned out exactly the way I thought they would, but I don't have any regrets."

"Once in a while, I feel sad about not passing along to my sons the traditions and holidays that I loved as a child," Kathy says, "and if we didn't have our own family traditions, I would regret giving up my childhood rituals. But our family life is full of holidays and rituals and traditions, and I can honestly say I'm happy, both for the kids and for myself."

Kathy continues, "Once someone asked me when I was going to stop pretending to be Jewish and either convert to Judaism or abandon the Jewish rituals and go back to church. But it's not a role to me. I'm not 'pretending' to be anything. I may not be a Jewish mother in name, but I am and always will be the mother of Jewish children. That's special to me, and I have no regrets."

Keith and Sari Grayson

Keith and Sari believe that their decision to combine Christianity and Judaism in their home was a good one. "As far as I'm concerned, this was the only logical choice," says Keith. "If both of us feel that our religions are important enough to us not to want to give them up, they're both important enough to pass on to our kids."

"Most of the Jewish/Christian couples we know are raising their kids the same way we are," says Sari. "The kids are fine. They're not mixed up or confused at all."

"The way I see it, Christianity and Judaism aren't contradictory," says Keith. "Judaism is based on the Ten Commandments, and Christianity is based on Judaism."

Sari adds, "It's not as if we were raising our kids half-Buddhist and half-Islamic. That would be ludicrous."

"People sometimes ask us whether either of us has ever thought about converting," says Keith. "It was never a serious consideration for either of us. I would never ask Sari to give up her religion. I love her the way she is, and Judaism is part of her. I know it's very meaningful to her, just as Christianity is meaningful to me. Combining both religions in our family eliminates the need for anyone to even think of converting."

"Besides," says Sari, "celebrating both religions is a lot of fun."

Heather echoes her mother. "I like being Christian and Jewish," she says. "You get to celebrate all the holidays that way."

"Of course, all she is interested in right now are the holidays," says Keith, "but we hope she'll appreciate other aspects of having two religions when she's older, like having been encouraged to grow up with an open mind and being knowledgeable about both traditions."

"I guess it's kind of good to have both religions," says Charles, "because you don't feel totally out of it when you go to a service or something. But religion's not a big deal to most of the guys I know."

While Heather is positive and Charles is neutral, Hannah is negative about her parents' decision to include both religions in their home. "They could have come to some kind of agreement if they'd wanted to," she says. "I resent that I was raised without a real religion."

"I can see Hannah's point," Sari concedes. "The kids don't

belong to one particular religion. Growing up Jewish gave me a sense of attachment and belonging, and maybe that's what Hannah feels she's missing."

"I know Hannah is pretty angry right now," says her father. "But she has to understand that we thought a lot about what we should do and we made what we felt was the best decision."

"I hope that Hannah will one day be able to see the positives in the way she was raised," says her mother. "I'd hate to think that she's going to see only the negatives all her life."

Do Keith and Sari have any regrets about their choice?

"The only thing I have some regrets about is that we did not give the kids rituals from both religions," says Keith. "I still think we could have had them both baptized and named in the synagogue. But we've already been through all that, and it's not worth reopening."

"I don't think that I have any regrets," says Sari, "but I am concerned about Hannah. She's so angry about not having a 'real religion.' Maybe she needs something different from what we gave her, or maybe we should have reacted differently to her questions when she was younger. I don't know."

"Or maybe it's just a phase," says Keith. "The other kids are fine. I'm proud of them. They're nice, well-behaved, ethical kids. I don't hear them saying terrible things about other people. They don't lie or steal. They're turning out fine. I don't think that we need to worry."

Comments

The Cohens and Graysons both see themselves as well-adjusted interfaith families. Each couple is satisfied with the choice they made and the way their children are growing up. As their parents planned, the Cohen boys are solidly rooted in Judaism, while the Grayson children are being exposed to elements of both Christianity and Judaism.

For the Cohens, helping their children establish a Jewish identity means giving them a formal Jewish education and participating with them in Jewish rituals. To Kathy, Judaism was attractive because "we could all participate in it together."

After taking part for several years in Jewish life both at home and in the temple, Kathy has come to see Judaism as "something special, even precious" that she and Sam are giving their children. Kathy values Jewish principles, traditions, and rituals and views her role as the mother of Jewish children as a special responsibility. By her own reckoning, Kathy has moved "more than halfway" toward conversion, although she may never choose Judaism for herself.

The Cohen boys are firmly anchored in Judaism. They are familiar with the history, values, and ethical principles that underlie Jewish thought and are forming an emotional attachment to Jewish rituals and traditions. What distinguishes Danny and Zeke from the Grayson children is that the Cohen boys not only understand their Jewish heritage, they feel they belong to it.

Because Keith and Sari felt that the traditions of both Christianity and Judaism were "important enough to pass on to the kids," they saw combining the two religions as the most logical option. Accordingly, they treat Christmas and Chanukah and Passover and Easter as essentially nonreligious family celebrations. They have introduced their children to Christian and Jewish rituals without having explored together the roots or substance of the holidays. They minimize the differences between Christian and Jewish ideology and emphasize the Judeo-Christian tradition.

Although Keith and Sari say they are comfortable with their blend of Judaism and Christianity, some family tension exists. Keith is still disappointed that none of the children was baptized or named in a synagogue, but he feels the issue is "not worth reopening." Keith and Sari say they are waiting for the children to ask about religion, but at the same time they are hoping that Hannah's questioning is "just a phase" that she is going through. Keith asserts that the children are "not missing anything," but Sari is aware that the children lack the "attachment and belonging" she remembers from her own Jewish childhood.

Whenever Keith and Sari encounter differences in their religious backgrounds and attitudes, they consistently retreat into the comfortable refrain "We did our best."

The children of both families seem to be well adjusted and normal. Keith could also be talking about the Cohen children when he says about his own, "They're nice, well-behaved, ethical kids." The difference lies in how the children see themselves. The Grayson children have an intellectual understanding of their Jewish and Christian roots but no sense of belonging to either religious group.

◆ ◆ ◆ ─────────────────────────────

Final Thoughts

Two years before our son was born, Ben and I made the commitment to raise Nathan as a Jew and to function as a Jewish family. We are satisfied with our decision. So far, almost everything has worked out the way we planned. Nathan is a Jew. He has the strong, positive Jewish identity that we wanted for him. He is part of Jewish communal life and identifies with Jewish history. As we had hoped, Nathan values Jewish art, music, food, literature, and traditions. Judaism provides us with the holidays and rituals that we wanted to observe as a family. But that is only part of our story.

We knew that Judaism had much to offer us but would also present challenges. The problems that we were able to predict, we met head-on. For Ben, the challenge was to be more observant than he had been for many years. He is Nathan's primary Jewish role model, assumes most of the responsibility for Nathan's Jewish education, and teaches both Nathan and me about Jewish culture and religious traditions.

I was challenged to learn to cook special holiday foods, follow the Jewish customs, and observe the Jewish rituals in my home. On a personal level, I tried to find ways to honor the Christian holidays without disrupting our Jewish household. Over the years, I have established certain personal ways to observe Christmas and Easter without bringing Christian symbols or traditions into our home. Ben and Nathan know that I go to church on Easter with my mother and that I spend Christmas morning with my parents. Both Ben and Nathan accept and respect my need for a Christian presence in my personal life, if not in my home.

Like all parents of Jewish children, Ben and I know that our son is probably going to encounter anti-Semitism at some time. Our response has been to try and give Nathan the tools to fight anti-Semitism, on both the personal and societal levels.

Until recently, Ben and I had not discussed whether we would continue practicing Jewish rituals and holidays after Nathan leaves home. Had we become a Jewish family solely for the purpose of introducing Nathan to Judaism and instilling him with its values, or will Judaism be a part of the fabric of our adult life? Will we remain active in the synagogue when Nathan goes away to college, or will I begin to attend church regularly? Will our grandchildren come to us for Jewish holidays? These are some of the issues that Ben and I talk about now, so that we will be better prepared to deal with them in the future.

The question of conversion recurs frequently. Before Nathan was born, I never seriously thought about adopting Judaism. But now that I have begun to feel welcome and valued in the Reform Jewish community and have become more involved in Jewish life, the possibility of conversion becomes less remote. Our family life would certainly be less complicated if I converted. If I were a Jew, there would be no limit to my participation in the synagogue and no question about my role in Nathan's bar mitzvah. If I converted, I would never have to explain to Nathan or anyone else why I chose to raise my son in a religion that I have not chosen for myself. Why, then, have I not converted?

At the heart of the matter are the distinctly Christian beliefs and rituals that retain a meaning and value to me. I find a special comfort in the Christian notion of heaven, even though I feel that Jewish mourning traditions are much more responsive to human needs than Christian funeral services are. I believe in the divinity of Jesus, even though it is difficult to justify that concept rationally. If I miss church on Christmas or

Easter, I experience an uneasy emptiness. No matter how much I respect Jewish values, ideology, and traditions, no matter how involved in Jewish communal life I become, I know that I would be denying an important part of myself if I were to convert to Judaism—at least right now.

The question of conversion recurs partly because the Reform movement is reaching out to non-Jewish congregants. Because I do not feel any pressure to choose Judaism, I am comfortable with my decision to leave the issue open for now. There may, however, come a time when conversion might be the right choice for me.

Our decision to raise Nathan as a Jew has yielded unexpected benefits. Being the parent of a Jewish child meant that I had to curtail my involvement in my church, and I worried about losing the friendships that I had made there and the sense of belonging that the church had given me. But our Reform synagogue has provided me with very much the same kind of community. It is committed to shared goals, respectful of personal religious beliefs, and dedicated to the religious education of the children. Ben, Nathan and I have all been included in the life of the congregation in a spirit of warm acceptance and respect.

I also did not expect that the cycle of Jewish holidays and rituals would become so ingrained in our family life. Even though we stay up until midnight on December 31, it is on Rosh Hashanah that we take stock of our lives and make our resolutions. Each Passover, we gauge Nathan's growth by his increasing proficiency in Hebrew. We begin our weekend time together by lighting Shabbat candles on Friday night. When we are on vacation, we take along our Shabbat on the Road kit: a pair of tiny candlesticks and birthday candles, a box of grape juice, and a package of saltine crackers. Even more than we thought they would, Jewish holidays and rituals regularly bring us together and strengthen our family ties.

One of our greatest satisfactions in raising Nathan as a Jew has been that Judaism offers Nathan a set of values that he understands and implements in his life. When I say that Nathan has developed a set of values, I do not mean that he is simply a nice person or that he has memorized a series of laws and is following them. Being nice and following rules are standards for socially acceptable behavior. They are not values.

Nor are values abstract beliefs. Believing in a principle and talking about it does not make that principle a value. Values are not beliefs about what constitutes moral behavior. Our values cause us to act. We help those in need because we believe that doing so is our responsibility. The belief motivates the action. If a belief is not strong enough to inspire action, it is not a value, no matter how often it is verbalized.

Many Jewish/Christian couples decide to teach their children values that are common to both their religions, often using the term "traditional Judeo-Christian values." It is true that both Judaism and Christianity regard honesty, truthfulness, kindness, and respect toward others as basic values. But because Judaism and Christianity are based on different views of God's relationship to people and of our role in the world, many of the values that Christianity and Judaism seem to share are, in reality, quite different. Whether or not Jewish and Christian parents are aware of the fact, they operate from different value systems.

A major difference between Christian and Jewish values is that one focuses on beliefs while the other is more action-oriented. The Christian values I was taught in Sunday school seemed otherworldly, difficult to grasp, abstract rather than concrete. The idea of "turning the other cheek" was foreign to my childish notion of justice. The directive to "love your enemy" was hard to understand and harder to follow. Not until my college years did I begin to grasp some of the basic Christian precepts.

In contrast, my eleven-year-old son already has a set of values that he articulates and practices. Nathan picks up trash and recycles cans because he understands the Jewish value of *tikkun olam*—to help heal, repair, and transform the world. He donates his own money to charity and gives his outgrown clothes and toys to a homeless shelter because Jews are responsible for giving *tzedakah*—sharing their resources with the less fortunate. At times he says a kind word or does a helpful deed not because he is looking for praise but because it is a mitzvah, a commandment. Doing right simply because it is right makes Nathan feel good about himself.

When we chose Judaism for Nathan, I was sure that it would provide him with a strong identity, a heritage, and a community. Since we made that decision, I have also come to appreciate the action-oriented nature of Jewish values. Nathan's value system is clearly the combined result of his formal religious training and our efforts to practice Jewish ethics in our family life. His value system is indistinguishable from his identity as a Jew. Hannah Grayson might say that by choosing Judaism as our family faith, we have provided Nathan with a religious hometown that he can call his own.

◆ ◆ ◆ ————————————————————————

Resources for Interfaith Couples from Reform Jewish Outreach

Through the Reform movement's Outreach program, Reform Jewish congregations throughout North America offer interfaith couples a place in which they are welcome to explore a Jewish connection for themselves and their children. The following publications, programs, and referral sources are available to assist couples.

PUBLICATIONS

Belin, David. "What Judaism Offers for You: A Reform Perspective," UAHC-CCAR Commission on Reform Jewish Outreach, 1991. This pamphlet is available from the UAHC regional Outreach offices at a charge of $2.00.

Einstein, Stephen J., and Lydia Kukoff. *Every Person's Guide to Judaism,* 1989.

Perelson, Ruth, and the UAHC Department for Religious Education. *Come Let Us Welcome Shabbat,* 1989. This kit, which includes a do-it-yourself booklet and an audiotape, is available for $12.95 from the UAHC Reform Curriculum Resource Center, 838 Fifth Avenue, New York, NY 10021.

Syme, Daniel. *The Jewish Home: A Guide for Jewish Living,* 1988.

Except as otherwise noted, all of the books listed on page 143 can be ordered from the UAHC Press, 838 Fifth Avenue, New York, NY 10021   212-249-0100.

PROGRAMS

Interfaith Couples Discussion Groups. These small-group discussion topics, titled "Times and Seasons," "Let's Talk," "Opening Doors," and "Yours, Mine and Ours," provide a forum for interfaith couples to explore, together with a trained facilitator, such questions as:

- What does my religion mean to me?
- How can we deal with the pressure from family and friends?
- Which holidays will we celebrate?
- How should we raise the kids?

These discussion programs take place on a weekly or monthly basis in many Reform temples or in a central location in major metropolitan areas and are sponsored by the Reform movement.

Introduction to Judaism Classes. Basic Judaism classes ranging in length from twelve to twenty-six weeks are conducted throughout the United States and Canada for interfaith couples and others who would like to learn the basics of Jewish traditions, beliefs, and practices. Students often participate in a Passover seder and a Sabbath celebration. A class may also include an introduction to Jewish history and prayer-book Hebrew. Many courses provide interfaith couples with the opportunity to discuss with other participants the special issues that they have encountered.

REFERRAL SOURCES

Call your local Reform congregation for information about the programs listed above, as well as for information about

other opportunities for interfaith couples and families in your community. Reform rabbis are available for counsel. They, along with other temple professional and lay leaders, will introduce you to congregants if that is your wish.

In addition, the Union of American Hebrew Congregations, the umbrella organization of Reform Jewish congregations in North America, has Outreach staff members in its thirteen regional offices throughout the United States and Canada. They can tell you about regional and city-wide programs, as well as programs in various nearby synagogues. They can also inform you about additional printed resources. For information about regional services, write to the Commission on Reform Jewish Outreach, 838 Fifth Avenue, New York, NY 10021, or call 212-249-0100.